Map

Second Edition
ISBN: 979-8-9854265-3-3
Cover photos by the author.

Grateful acknowledgement is given for permission to reprint lyrics from the following:

"Sure Thing" written by Kristen Hall and Michelle Malone. Copyright © 1990 Sony/ATV Songs LLC, Cold Cocked Music, Kristen Hall. All rights on behalf of Sony/ATV Songs LLC administered by Sony/ATV Music Publishing LLC, 8 Music Square West, Nashville, TN 37203. All rights reserved. Used by permission.

"The Other Side of the Wood" written by Fred Small. Copyright © 1993 Pine Barrens Music (BMI). Used by permission.

Language Or The Kiss
Words and Music by Emily Saliers
© 1994 EMI VIRGIN SONGS, INC. and GODHAP MUSIC
All Rights Controlled and Administered by EMI VIRGIN SONGS, INC.
All Rights Reserved International Copyright Secured Used by Permission

"Walk of Shame" written by Mike Phillips, Eddie Matz, and Peter Kim for performance by Pennsylvania Six-5000 and adapted to align with a character's pseudonym. Copyright © 1993 Mike Phillips, Eddie Matz, and Peter Kim. Used by permission.

I knew a girl
who wanted to write a lovestory
because she hadn't read any she liked.

This is for her, and for all of us

Map
a memoir

Audrey Beth Stein

map: an imperfect, incomplete, representation of a terrain. A map does not replace a journey, and what follows is merely how I often remember where I've been. Most names have been changed.

I Want a Girlfriend

November 1996
Senior Year
University of Pennsylvania, Philadelphia PA

My friend Matthew calls me as I'm heading out the door. *Did you mean what you said last week?*

At first I'm not sure what he's talking about.

Did you mean what you said, about wanting a girlfriend?

Why are you asking?

Because there's someone I want to fix you up with.

I don't want to be fixed up. I want things to happen. Then I ask, *Who?*

Her name's Marcie Roberts, he says. *I don't think you know her.*

Does Matthew really think I'm *that* unattractive? That I'm *compatible* with Marcie Roberts? Her whole presence exudes insecurity. Why doesn't Matthew think I'm good enough to be with someone hot? Someone other people lust after. Someone who has her shit together, who has ex-girlfriends. Someone who doesn't need to scream *hi I'm gay* to the *Daily Pennsylvanian,* which is how I know who Marcie Roberts is in the first place.

No thanks, I tell Matthew. *I'm not interested.*

When I said *I want a girlfriend,* I meant I wanted one in that moment—a moment precipitated by watching the lesbian film *Go Fish* and developing an immediate crush on Guinevere Turner's character Max.

I want a girlfriend like the one in my dream last week, where we were roommates first, and friends, and then we kissed once just like that and it was all affectionate and we kept going, and in the middle I asked *wanna live together?* and she laughed because we already did and kissed me again. That's what I want. The holding hands, the friendship that blurs into more. Not Matthew fixing me up.

Not: having to admit my fears, having to declare a sexual orientation as a prerequisite. Not: having to be vulnerable in order to get there.

Are you sure? Matthew asks.

Yeah, I say. I might be wrong about Marcie Roberts, but I need to trust my gut.

When I stop at Chats a little while later for something to eat, AJ from my favorite Penn *a cappella* group is behind the counter. She takes my order, then asks me, *How did the yearbook pictures from our last concert come out?*

Good, I tell her, pleased that she recognized me. *I wish I had copies of the contact sheets to show you.* My mind drifts back to the performance. AJ had been totally immersed in the music and *radiating* joy, and I'd just kept shooting away until my film ran out, trying to photograph that joy.

AJ and I start talking, and when she has to wait on customers I step to the side and write. I don't have paper with me, so I use a Chats napkin to write on.

When you're drunk, whatever you say isn't so loaded, I write on the napkin. I write backwards to reach the creative parts of my brain. It's a trick I learned from a guy in a homeless shelter,

MAP   3

where I was volunteering one high school Christmas. He said he could tell from my body language that I was lefty, and he'd heard that left-handers could write backwards, and did I have a pen so we could try it out? Mirror-image backwards, he meant, so that afterwards if you hold the blank side of the page up to the light you can read what you wrote.

When I'm drunk, I write, *things mean just what they mean and not ten things underneath.*

I can count the number of times I've been drunk on one hand. Last night would be the ring finger. *Underage drinking is illegal,* my mom would say, *and don't think I'm going to bail you out if you get arrested.* My parents rarely drink anything beyond the sip of Manischevitz required for Shabbat *kiddush.* For me, drinking is a very conscious choice each time, a *decision* to relinquish that bit of control.

There's this haircut I want, I write, *shorter than my normal just-above-shoulder-length haircut, but long enough that someone can run their fingers through it. I want it to be so cool that this girl in my history class will decide she's not straight.* When I told people this at a party last night, I was drunk, so that's all it meant. Not like telling Matthew when I'm sober that I want a girlfriend.

AJ asks what I'm writing so I read her part of it, skipping the section about the girl in my history class, and then she tries writing backwards on her own napkin. She's concentrating and kind of laughing, and from my angle she looks like Claire Danes in *My So-Called Life.* Crinkled forehead, wisp of hair falling in her eyes. Interestingly complex and thoughtful and smart. Good looking in a way that's definitely feminine but comes through equally well in a Chats t-shirt and jeans or in a slinky black dress. Me, I haven't been able to pull off feminine since puberty started. Today I'm in my favorite overalls and a jester cap.

This is hard, AJ says, frowning at the blue inkmarks on her napkin.

Try holding the napkin up to your forehead, I suggest. AJ looks at me quizzically, but I demonstrate and then she follows my lead, writing *My Name is AJ* in perfect mirror writing.

She places her napkin on the counter next to mine and compares the two. *Neat. Your turn,* she says, handing me the pen.

I lean on the counter and no interesting phrases come to mind so I write *Four score and seven years ago.* My hand shapes the letters easily.

You do it fast, AJ observes. *Do you write like this a lot?*

It's because I'm lefty, I explain, and tell her about the guy in the homeless shelter.

AJ gestures to someone behind me and I realize I'm blocking a customer. I step aside.

Pretending I'm looking through my camera, I watch AJ. She's making a burrito, so she won't notice me. *Indisputably cool* is the phrase that comes to mind as she sings along unselfconsciously to the tape in the background. AJ has the only kind of coolness I've ever envied. It's the kind that comes from having your interests and passions fit naturally within the norms defined by your peers--so you can be cool and still be true to yourself.

I know, intellectually, that being true to myself is more important than being cool, but I want the spoils of coolness, too. I want to be able to enter a room full of people and not be awkward, want heads to turn, want to seduce and then say *no thanks.* Sometimes I see couples and I want to be them, not me with either of them, but them with each other. I want to know what it is to be a beautiful person having sex with a beautiful person. What it is to be desired as you walk down the street, to

MAP 5

be intimidating, to be able to say *hey what's up* in high school and not just pass for cool momentarily but actually feel it.

Once the customer is gone, I go back up to the counter and AJ and I start talking about music. Our tastes overlap but AJ also listens to a lot of musicians I've never heard.

You should make me a mix, I propose, *and I'll make you one.* She likes the idea and writes her phone number on my napkin. I brush the front point of my jester cap out of my face the way people brush their hair away. I remember some article about how women playing with their hair is a sign of attraction.

That evening my friend Derek, a fellow writer who graduated last year, calls from Colorado to tell me he and his girlfriend got engaged. When he calls, I'm lying on my bed staring at the backwards blue letters on the quote board on my wall—*I didn't say I was gay, I said I was in love.* The quote comes from the movie *The Incredibly True Adventures of Two Girls in Love,* which I watched in the theater during the summer after sophomore year. As I stood on line for a ticket, I'd wondered, *will people think I'm gay just for being here? Are they all making assumptions about me?* I'd blasted the soundtrack until school began again, grateful for the way that movies let you try on new identities.

Maybe it's the distance, or the phone factor, maybe just knowing he's not a part of my day-to-day life anymore even though he's a good friend, but it's easy to talk to Derek. *How do you know you're straight?* I ask him, hoping that will give me clues. I guess I'm looking for him to say he never questioned it, admit that he doesn't know, but his answer surprises me. He tells me he's given serious thought to men.

Really? I ask. *And?*

Nothing. I mean I can appreciate a guy being attractive, sure, but beyond that, nothing. He tells me all this matter-of-factly, that of course he's thought about it, how could he know for sure he was straight if he hadn't?

I'm not sure, I admit to him. *About myself, I mean.*

This is what I'm afraid of people around here knowing, that I'm not sure. That I'm not as confident as I appear to be, and that this particular realm—sexuality—is my Achilles heel. I envy the people who know they're gay when they're teenagers, who have crushes on their bunkmates at camp and the person with the locker next to theirs in middle school gym class. I envy Matthew even though he had to wrestle with it in college—depression and therapy and everything—because he had the feeling deep down as soon as puberty hit. It seems like anyone who's gay and comes out is *sure,* they've known and repressed it for a long time before saying anything. But me?

Junior year another friend asked me directly, *do you think you're gay?* and I just didn't know how to answer. If I knew, I'd be out. But I have all these mixed up feelings inside, all these pieces which don't quite fit. Does it *have* to mean something that when I was six I stole my dad's deck of cards featuring photographs of nude women and hid in my closet studying each and every card? I've been attracted to guys for as long as I can remember. I spent two whole summers fighting feelings for my Tom Cruise look-alike counselor that were too strong to be labeled a mere crush. That can't just not count, can it?

The big question is more than *what am I?* It's *why haven't I figured it out already?* I've always been identified as the smart one, the one who understands everything first. My mom brags about how well I know myself the way some parents brag about

MAP   7

their kids' soccer trophies. So how come this big piece is still a mystery to me?

You should hook up with a chick, Derek advises before we hang up, like it's that easy.

Something To Share

I get in the habit of stopping by Chats a few times a week, and AJ seems glad to have the company, keeping me up-to-date on her work schedule and suggesting when it's busy that I plan a study break to coincide with her work break. I'm definitely attracted to her, and my pulse quickens whenever she enters my sight. Conversation is easy. I want to make a move, ask her out. I can imagine it this time, imagine the words rolling off my tongue that usually get stuck in my throat—if only she would give me a sign. But a suave *will you go out with me?* in the middle of Chats could backfire if she's only interested in guys.

The next month passes quickly, with a paper or presentation due every week. I'm juggling five classes and a part-time job, and I'm spending more time online, partly because it's easier to spend ten minutes answering an email than a couple of hours hanging out with a friend on campus. Meals come mainly from the food trucks and Indian restaurants which line Penn's campus. Relaxation comes in small doses: photographing *a cappella* shows and football games, reading my stories Saturday nights at the Writers House open mic, and occasionally biking downtown for a change of scene. Study breaks at Chats with AJ become an integral part of my paper-writing routine, and as we get to

MAP   9

know each other better, I learn there's a guy in the picture. Near the end of finals week, I go to AJ's apartment off-campus to pick up the mix she's made me.

I'm sprawled across the hardwood floor of her bedroom. *Have you ever been in love?* I ask her.

I think I'm falling in love with the guy I'm seeing now, AJ confides, *and I don't want to be falling in love with him. It sucks.*

AJ's sitting cross-legged on her second-hand desk chair, hair pinned up, sticking the A and B labels on my mix tape. She tells me how the guy she's seeing got jealous when she went out with another guy, even though the first guy is up in Vermont and they agreed to see other people. I tell her that I'm not seeing anyone, that I've never been in love, that I kind of dated this guy Jake a couple of years ago who said he was falling in love with me. I leave out the details. I only mentioned Jake so she'll think I have experience, so I have *something* to share. If I tell details, I'll be admitting, *it wasn't much of anything.*

It was my sophomore year, Jake and Matthew's freshman year. They had been best friends in high school, and Jake and I met when he came up one weekend to visit Matthew. Jake and I hit it off immediately, talking for a couple of hours in the hallway while Matthew slept in. We emailed a couple of times and then towards the end of spring break he called from Matthew's house in New Jersey to see if I wanted to hang out.

Is Matthew coming? I asked, and Jake hesitated on the phone.

Did you want him to? Jake asked. *I think he has other plans.*

It turned out that Matthew didn't have plans, but somehow it still wound up being just me and Jake that night. Jake showed up with a bouquet of flowers, and that's when I knew for sure that he intended it to be a date. It would be my first official date since skipping stones at the camp lake one Shabbat when I was twelve.

Jake and I walked around South Street for a while before stopping somewhere for dinner. I felt strange in my body, which was taller and bulkier than Jake's. The awareness of being on a date overlay what otherwise felt like a nice evening with a new friend. *I brought chocolate,* Jake said as we finished our entrees. He'd gotten two kinds, a raspberry and a bittersweet. He told me he'd asked the chocolate store guy to recommend *a good chocolate, and a good chocolate to share with a date.*

You've probably figured it out by now, Jake said, *but I like you a lot. I've been thinking about you since we met.*

I envied Jake for his forthrightness, for the ability to admit exactly how he felt. I'd spent most of the year in an unspoken crush on someone from my writing class, lacking that ability. The check came then, delaying the need for a response. I was full from dinner, so Jake hung onto the chocolates until we were heading back, and then he asked which to open. My taste buds wanted the raspberry one—the date one—but I said the bittersweet.

It was late as we walked back, and Jake seemed too tired to drive home safely, so I invited him to crash in my room. *Let's stop at my car,* he said, as we neared the dorm. *I have pajamas and a toothbrush and stuff. Don't take it the wrong way, I brought my sleeping bag, too, I just thought it might be late to drive back.*

I hadn't taken it the wrong way at all, pegging Jake as less experienced than me, and he stayed over that night in a sleeping bag on my floor. We shared a solid hug goodnight and the next morning a quick kiss on the lips goodbye. After he left I emailed the guy from my writing class I still had a crush on, *I had a date*

MAP   11

last night but I'm not sure if I'm interested or not. Hoping that Jake's interest would prompt the guy to ask me out himself. His response was inconclusive, complaining about not getting dates, and I was still too chicken to write back *how about me?*

A week later, Jake drove up to Philly with a couple of friends to check on Matthew. This was in the beginning of Matthew's pre-coming-out depression, though I didn't know it at the time. When Matthew hadn't shown up at Jake's campus as promised and wasn't answering his phone, Jake had gotten worried enough to make the drive. Matthew wasn't in his room when Jake and his friends arrived. Jake's friends went to check the common rooms, and Jake knocked on my door. Jake and I wound up lying on my bed, kissing and a little more, hard bulge under his jeans against my khakis, and it felt good.

This is the first place I've wanted to be, all week, Jake said, *and the last place I ever thought I would.*

I liked the physical part, wanted that to happen again, but didn't want to get emotionally involved. I'd already made a rule about not dating freshmen, because I didn't want to go through that adjustment period more than once. Jake, a high school underachiever now stuck at an unchallenging college, envied Matthew and I our intellectually-stimulating environment and had his heart set on transferring to Penn. I sensed him seeing me in particular as the light in his dark freshman tunnel, and I was wary.

After that night I flirted with Jake over email, hinting about our tongues moving over each other's skin. I enjoyed the occasional emails and didn't think about him much in between. I was busy making arrangements to stay in Philly and write that summer, a plan that felt crucial to my future—create stories good enough to send to publishers, complete a draft of the novel

I'd started two years earlier, learn how far my talents could take me. Then, over email, I found out Jake wasn't a virgin.

I panicked.

I'd had fun so far, but did I really want this? Did I really like Jake? I was terrified I'd do something stupid, something with repercussions I couldn't handle. The chorus of a Penn *a cappella* song called *Walk of Shame* kept running through my head. *Jägermeister and Bacardi made her fuck a freshman dork named Jake.* What if I didn't say *no*, what if my body was stronger than my will?

Jake was smitten, hard. I liked that he told me where he stood, but it was also daunting, requiring a definitiveness on my part I didn't have. *If it's orgasm you want, I know of more than one way,* he said over email. He wrote about taking it slow, *no means no and yes means maybe,* but he also wrote about always carrying a condom with him, being prepared, and I wasn't.

That fall I hadn't been prepared, with the tutor. I try not to think about that. Or how much worse it could have been.

Soon after our talk about taking it slow, Jake asked over email, *will you spend weekends this summer on my parents' boat, just you and me? You could write and I could do my summer school homework during the day, and then we'd spend time together in the evening.*

I tried to imagine it, tempted by the idyllic image of relaxing with Jake by the water after a full week of writing, but I knew it wouldn't be like that. No way could I write with Jake in my head. There wasn't room for anything that summer but me and my writing.

I have to write my novel, I replied, thinking maybe I could allow myself one low-key visit. *Please don't drag me down. Can you fly with me?*

MAP   13

Jake emailed back saying, *I'll try. I may be falling in love with you. I'll take what I can get.*

I got drunk that weekend and smoked my first joint. *I need to try a new vice,* I told my friends. *If I don't do this I'll sleep with Jake, I know I will and I don't want to.* I don't know how I came to that logic, but it felt accurate and I got drunk and I got high and I wrote big frantic journal entries about how I wanted to get off the rollercoaster and I started to feel a little calmer, the threat of sex with Jake and all it could destroy temporarily abating.

Then a letter from Jake arrived. Nothing special, just a letter, but after reading it, I tore it to shreds. Just its arrival in my mailbox had disrupted the tenuously safe space for my writing that I'd barely begun to create. *I'm sorry Jake,* I wrote him on email. *I've gotta do my own thing this summer, no strings. Talk to me next September, maybe then.*

When September rolled around, Jake was already involved with his current girlfriend, and I was wrapped up in my book and another fruitless crush. I went off to Israel in the spring and Jake emailed me, *I understand what you meant way back when about not dating freshmen, it's my rule now too.*

Wanting to change the subject before AJ starts asking me about Jake, I gesture to the painting above her dresser and ask, *did you make that?*

Yeah, she says. She reaches behind her desk and pulls out a painting of a woman with long dark hair and a familiar necklace.

Is that you? I ask. The woman looks self-conscious, uncertain, features out of proportion, not beautiful and confident like the AJ I see.

It's new, she says, nodding. *I'm not sure if I like it.*

I think about how different it is from my own self-portraits. I try to be honest in my photographs but also show the beauty I feel inside, the beauty I feel most when I'm writing or making a photograph or soaking up nature, beauty that rarely shows up in other people's snapshots of me. The self-portrait I chose to put on my website captures me in thought and action, writing on my jeans because the muse found me without paper. Other people's snapshots mostly show my profile, the overbite and bad posture, the glasses jutting out and the pointy forward-curl my hair makes no matter what I do. I tried contacts once but I couldn't put my finger in my eye.

AJ shows me a couple of watercolors, and then I flip through her CD collection, pausing at the Indigo Girls' *Rites of Passage* album. There's a picture on the back of the liner of Emily—one of the two Indigo Girls—with her hands behind her neck, wearing jeans and a turtleneck with the sleeves pushed up, thick black belt. *She's hot,* I say. *The way Emily's holding her body in this picture.* AJ comes over and examines it. I don't usually think of Emily as being hot, but the photo fascinates me, how she's wearing clothes the way I do—covering herself—and yet her body language is daring you to come find out what's underneath.

Do you still date guys? AJ asks, handing me back the CD. I'm not even consciously aware of what she knows. It's come up in little pieces, in that low-key learning-about-a-new-friend way. The same way I found out that she hates olives and she's kind of dating this guy in Vermont.

I like that she makes this assumption that I date, that it's this activity that I do.

I haven't dated anyone in a while, I say. *Not since Jake. It sucks not knowing how I'm going to end up. I don't know if I'm ever going*

MAP   15

to have to deal with things like anti-gay marriage laws personally, or just have my sexuality be irrelevant.

Do you know which you're looking for? AJ asks. I shake my head.

I want to ask AJ about herself, but I don't. I know this could be my window of opportunity, but her friendship is becoming more important to me, and I don't want to mess that up. Or so I tell myself, wondering if for once it's the truth. Would I really have asked her out last month, if she'd hinted? Would I now?

You May Have Inferred This

Sexuality, I type. *You may have inferred this already, but now you're going to get it straight—no pun intended. I've been questioning for a while. And it's been so nice to be able to talk openly with people online from the Indigo Girls Mailing List without having to make any declarative statements. Much easier than trying to talk about it with people who have known me for years.* I press *send* and delete old emails while waiting for my friend Tyler's reply. I'm supposed to be packing to go home tomorrow, not emailing.

Tyler's a freshman at Penn, and we met in November through the Indigo Girls email list. We call occasionally and have met in person a couple of times to watch Indigo Girls videos and trade bootlegs, but email remains our most common form of communication. I know she's online because almost immediately there's another email in my box.

So what have you decided? Tyler asks. *Do you agree with what you concluded in your biology paper about everyone having the capability to be attracted to and fall in love with another specific person, irrespective of gender?*

Yeah, I respond to Tyler, *I do.*

I type and erase and retype the next part, try to sound nonchalant. Trying to be clear, but nonchalant.

MAP   17

Which makes me bi, I guess, by the common definition of the word. Thus far I'm non-practicing. As for the closet, I've decided it's just not going to be a part of my life. In or out. I don't like the whole concept—how did I get there? Or the notion that it's up to me to come out—why am I assuming that all these people are assuming I'm straight? If I'm asked, I'll be honest, but I'm not into billboards.

When we first met, Tyler writes back, *Heather said you couldn't be bisexual, because why would you be writing a paper about yourself?*

Heather is another person from the Indigo Girls list. Tyler writes to her a lot, I think, but I've only interacted with her the night we all met in person and watched Indigo Girls videos together. I laugh, then type *laughing out loud* in email shorthand. *LOL! I guess I was writing to find out if I was writing about myself.*

Hee hee, Tyler responds. *I don't really feel comfortable going into detail about myself yet...but suffice it to say I agree that everyone can fall in love regardless of gender.*

Tyler and I keep emailing for a while, gossiping about a couple of people from the list who she thinks might be dating, as I try to pack. My journal goes in first, in its own easy-to-get-to pocket, then bras and underwear and a pair of boots. I have jeans at home and I can borrow Dad's shirts when mine run out. I collect the dozen heavy books and notebooks I'll need to finish my incomplete History paper and make sure there's room for my Powerbook case, which I'll pack in the morning. The Tom Paxton CD I'm giving Dad for Chanukah and the new-in-paperback Amy Tan book for Mom can go in the front pocket of the Powerbook case, and there's still space in this trekking-around-Israel backpack for some tapes—AJ's mix, an Indigo Girls bootleg, Mary Chapin Carpenter's *Shooting Straight In the Dark.*

I can barely lift my backpack, I write to Tyler. *Why haven't they built that high-speed monorail between my living room and Thirtieth Street Station yet??*

LOL! Tyler writes. *I think it's next on the list after the one between my room and Paris.*

There's another email in my box from someone on the Indigo Girls list wanting to read my biology paper, so I press *reply* and send it, inviting her to give feedback. I've been vague about my sexuality when posting to the list itself, letting people draw their own conclusions, but in the one-on-one exchanges prompted by my bio paper, I've gotten into conversations about the Kinsey scale and about the lack of scientific knowledge about bisexuality, and someone even told me about what it was like when her father came out to her family.

I'm planning to tell *my* parents about my sexuality sometime this vacation. Casually. Just in case. Let them know that me getting involved with a woman is a possibility, so if it ever does happen, telling them won't be a bigger deal than telling them I'm involved with a guy.

Around midnight Tyler writes, *Please don't email me anymore tonight. I have to finish a ten page paper by 9 AM, and email keeps distracting me.*

Okay, I type, *I won't email you anymore. But why don't you just LOGOUT?*

You mean it's possible to logout? she blitzes right back.

I dial her phone number and get the machine—I guess she's serious about getting work done. I listen to the chorus of an Indigo Girls song and a long beep then leave a message. *Tyler, I think I'm gonna have to enroll you in Emailers Anonymous.*

I check my email a couple of minutes later and there's another message from her. *I'm taking you with me,* she says. *I can*

MAP   19

just see it now. Hi, I'm Tyler, and I'm an email addict. This is Audrey, and she's an addict too. Then we could get out of that stupid meeting really quickly and go check our email.

Coming out, the way it always seems to be portrayed in books and movies, the way Matthew experienced it—the deep dark secret, the internal agony, the fear that your whole world could come crashing down—that, for me, isn't about sexuality. Coming out like that, for me, was about picking my nose. *I pick my nose.* Said on the phone to a good friend when I was eighteen, terrified. I was crying, shaking even, in relief and shock and so much else at her so unexpected response, *That's your big secret? That's normal, I do that all the time.* Following so many years of not knowing, of thinking it was wrong, *I* was wrong, something was horribly wrong with me, because I picked my nose and no matter how often my parents said *Audrey, stop that! use a tissue!* I couldn't make myself stop. I'd misunderstood those words at age—what? four? five? three?—to mean *that's wrong, that's bad,* even *that's unnatural,* rather than *that's not polite to do in public,* and there was nothing anywhere to teach me the truth.

In elementary school, even the younger kids would taunt me on the playground: *Audrey Stein is doing it doing it doing it, picking her nose and chewing it chewing it chewing it.* It didn't matter how long it had been since I'd actually been caught—the taunts followed me. To my parents, the private school I entered in sixth grade meant a better education. To me it meant no one knew me, no one would ever have to know I picked my nose. But the relief came with a new fear: *would these people still be my friends if they knew?* I was terrified someone would find out and it would all be over. I remember thinking in high school, *it would be easier if I were gay instead. There are books on that, there are other people.* I got to college and immediately performed furtive searches in Penn's online card catalog and medical databases. Nothing was listed under *nosepicking,* but I eventually convinced myself it had to be some sort of medical condition—perhaps a form of obsessive-compulsive disorder?—which meant as soon as I could find the guts to tell someone, I could be cured.

During my freshman year winter break, on the phone with my friend Laurette, I came out. *I pick my nose.*

As I'm getting dressed on my first morning home, my mom calls out to me from the bathroom, *Audrey, you need to get your book out of here, unless you want it to get wet.* I pull on jeans and go into the bathroom, where Mom is wearing rubber gloves and exercise clothes and squirting Soft Scrub onto a sponge. My book's resting on the sink counter, face down, open to the page where I left off after my bath. *Tasting Life Twice: Literary Lesbian Fiction.*

Are you reading that for class? Mom asks.

No, I say. *Someone from the Indigo Girls mailing list recommended it to me.* I pick up the book and fold down the corner of the page as a bookmark.

Is it good? She's wiping down the faucet and the underside of the soap dish.

Yeah, so far.

What makes it lesbian fiction?

My mom has a knack for asking the questions I'm still wrestling with myself. *I don't know,* I answer. *I've only read a few stories, I haven't figured it out. You can borrow it when I'm done.*

I'm still trying to get through the set of Toni Morrison books I bought last summer, Mom says, and then she starts talking to me about the one she just finished, *The Bluest Eye.*

MAP   21

Telling Mom casually isn't as easy as I expected.

Telling Dad isn't either. On Tuesday after dinner, my dad gives me a tour of the new computer program he's creating to put our family tree on the web. The page for me is simple—an only child of two living parents. I supply Dad with names of relatives I uncovered in my childhood genealogy research. While I go to my room to find the green notebook with even more relatives' names, my dad continues programming, and when I come back, he shows me the new trick he just added: now, if you check off *male,* the program will automatically give you a prompt for *wife* and if you check off *female* it will give a prompt for *husband.*

That's a neat trick, Dad, I say, *but don't you think you're forgetting something?*

What am I forgetting? he asks.

How can he be so oblivious? Mom wouldn't be. I give him a clue. *What about people who aren't legally married?*

He still doesn't get it. He looks confused like it will be too complicated to program and he can't think of anyone like that in our family anyway so he'll just leave it out. I wish I didn't have to mess up his code, but I want a space in this program no matter who I wind up with. Girl or boy or no one at all.

Well you can't assume everyone in the family is straight, I say. I want to say *I mean I'm not straight* but I chicken out and instead I just leave the room before either of us has to say anything else.

I log on to my email account and there's a post to the Indigo Girls Mailing List from this woman Catrina. I've pegged her as one of the cool people on the list—she's funny and lesbian and she posts regularly without crossing the line into Indigo Girls psycho-fan-dom. She says she's stuck at home with her parents in this little hick town in Washington state and she just graduated and she's bored and she wishes people would write to her to relieve her boredom. She's offering a free bootleg tape of last year's show at Bumbershoot to anyone who knows how to pronounce the name of her hick town, just spell it back phonetically over email. I don't know how to say the name of the town, and I already traded Tyler for that bootleg, but I don't want to get into a conversation with my parents right now, or write my history paper which is what they think I'm doing holed up in front of my computer, so I press *reply* and start writing.

To: Catrina
Date: Tue, 24 Dec 1996 23:40:12 -0500 (EST)

What is your Favorite Holiday? What were you studying in college? Where is your life heading? Are you happy?....What is your favorite crayola crayon color, and did you know there's no indigo in the old box of 64. Perhaps you could call around and find out if it exists in the 96 set, and if not we should start a campaign...it IS after all one of the colors of the rainbow. When did you join the list? How did you discover the Indigo Girls? Have you ever met anybody famous? Are you famous? Do you own a swiss army knife, an orange shirt, or a $5 guitar? How many Martians does it take to change a light bulb? (The answer is 1 1/2....are you laughing yet?) What is your favorite book today? If you could relive any one day in its entirety, what day would it be and why?

You don't have to answer all my questions....just enough to Relieve Your Boredom.

I press *send* and listen to the sounds of my dad starting to

MAP   23

vacuum and my mom yelling at him not to forget to use the little attachment to get *under* the couch this time. I pull out the books I need for my paper and try to think about the question, which is a vague *what do all these historical bestsellers have to do with each other?* but I have all these other questions which are unrelated and much more pressing. *Is just being honest to myself enough? Do I have to act on my feelings? How? Why would I choose a woman if I could be happy with a man?* Being open to the possibility and honest about my feelings is a lot different from actively seeking out a same-sex relationship in an intoler-ant society. I don't even know how I would begin looking, but I feel like something will be missing in my life if I get married and I've never had that deep emotional no-holds-barred relationship with a woman.

My dad knocks on my door and asks if I want to help him with the vacuuming. *No thanks,* I say. *I'm working on my history paper.*

No Holds Barred

To: Tyler
Subject: i need to talk to you
Date: Fri, 3 Jan 1997 15:43:06 -0500 (EST)

tyler, i hope you read this soon because i gotta talk to someone and you are the only person i know in flesh and blood who will understand.

i have been emailing catrina since the day before christmas. between what i sent her and what she sent me there are about two-hundred and nine messages over an eleven day period. i am falling in love with her. i am completely serious, i retract everything bad i ever said about people beginning relationships over the net. and yes, it is mutual, she is falling in love with me too. we are being rational about it, since we might not even be attracted to each other in real life, but that possibility scares the shit out of me. i have never been in love before, tyler. it is wonderful and frightening and terrible and perfect all in one. and she just left for her apartment in olympia this afternoon so we can't email again until she gets a working monitor for her computer there. we are going to try to talk on sunday though, and snail mail. god, i can't believe this is happening. and i can't friggin

24

MAP   25

tell people, tell them what, i'm in love with a woman i've never even met. but you know the list, and you know catrina through the list, and you know me, you know this can really happen, and i am not crazy, it is just so odd and new.

help me be rational, tyler, i think i am nearly about to explode. if i go west now it will either not work out and i will be severely bummed, or it will work out and i will not come back east to finish penn, which would ultimately probably doom the thing anyway. so now i gotta get through the next five months and maybe more without going nuts. what am i saying? i am already nuts. i am in love with catrina simone riley and she is an email address three time zones away. jesus.

I linger on the last sentences for a moment, absorbing the words I just wrote, realizing that Tyler may not get the email until vacation ends. My Powerbook and modem don't take up much physical space, yet they transform my large bedroom, drawing focus away from the familiar bookshelves and messy floor and the basket full of stuffed animals. It doesn't matter that a photograph of Mom and me wearing pajama bottoms on our heads like bunny ears is tacked up on my bulletin board, right next to the best-friends-for-life card Sasha gave me in third grade. It doesn't matter that there's a stack of books piled on my desk, waiting for me to incorporate them into my unfinished history paper. My attention is focused on the screen, a contemporary doorway to *somewhere else* made up of binary code and pixels of light.

Catrina's first email had arrived like any other email, courier-font letters *you have new mail* triggering the miniature spurt of adrenaline that often accompanies the unknown. *Oh good, I'm glad someone wrote me,* she began. *My favorite holiday is my birthday. Which will probably become a national holiday when I get famous. I'm not famous yet, but I figure eventually I will be, I'm not sure for what yet. Probably just for being me. My favorite book is The Color Purple, and not just because I like purple. Jeesz, how could indigo not be a color? If it ever stops snowing here I'll go down to the store and break open a box of ninety-six Crayolas myself.*

I had been going online a few times a day while taking breaks from writing my paper. I was corresponding with maybe half a dozen people from the Indigo Girls list, plus reading and occasionally responding to the plethora of list posts, but pretty soon it was Catrina's emails I was logging on for. She was snowbound in her parents' house and spending at least as much time online as I was, so there would almost always be a new message from her whenever I checked my email. I'm not sure how we began joking about getting married, but later that week she sang me *I'm a little teapot* over email and ended the serenade with *I loves you! Now will you marry me?*

Of course, I wrote back, and we started planning what we would wear for the wedding. We named our kid Zoe. In our dozen emails back-and-forth each night, we discussed religion and education and taking out the trash and how we would make up after our first fight with heartfelt apologies and then kissing and sex. It started to feel like more than just a joke. Even though I knew, *knew,* it was just email, knew we were three thousand miles away from each other.

Attraction is such a weird thing, Catrina wrote me yesterday evening. *I mean, I would love it if you lived in Washington and this*

MAP   27

would work for real, but who knows if we would be attracted to each other?

Of course we would be attracted to each other, I wrote back immediately, ending the sentence with a smiley face. But then I wrote, more seriously, *yeah, attraction is strange. I'm often surprised by who I'm attracted to. And sometimes with guys, I've been attracted and repulsed at the same time.* I thought about a guy in Israel who seemed kind of dorky and boring at first, and then once I knew him, his dorky parts became endearing and I decided he was hot. And I thought about a friend at Penn who I was intellectually drawn to but not attracted to physically, and how uncomfortable it made me to imagine becoming romantically involved with him. *I guess if we weren't attracted to each other,* I told Catrina, *we'd just hang out a lot. It does suck that we're on opposite coasts.*

Catrina and I had three email conversations going at once, so after I pressed *send* I went on to her next email. *How do you see yourself in the future?* she had asked. *With a man or with a woman? By the way, the road finally cleared up, so I'm going back to Olympia tomorrow, and so I won't have email until I can afford a new monitor.*

I reflected on her question for a while, writing and deleting, then the dinner bell rang and I typed quickly, as though I'd just received her email, *I'll answer you in about an hour, I have to eat dinner. Don't disappear on me or anything.*

How did I see myself in the future? Alone. I hated it, but for as long as I could remember, it had seemed inevitable: when Mom and Dad died, I would be left all alone. Even coming out about picking my nose hadn't changed that fear—though my friendships felt like they had a more solid base, I couldn't see a path leading from my fruitless attractions to a significant other. But now? Could it be possible?

I still have no idea, I told Catrina after dinner, thinking as I wrote. *It's so hard to envision. I could never see myself with kids, but even that's changing a little. I think I might be able to have kids with a woman, because then I wouldn't have to be the mom. I can't really see myself as a mom.*

That's fine, Catrina wrote back. *I'll be the mom. And you'll be the writer, and we'll be there when you need love, and we'll interrupt you when we need love back.*

I could feel myself near tears as I read her words. This was a life that had felt so unattainable for so long, so far out of reach I hadn't dared even imagine, and now it felt so perfect. Love and a family and writing and space. My fingers shook as I typed back, *I love you so much. But what if we're not attracted to each other?*

We can still grow old together, she said, *we'll just have lots of torrid affairs.*

I felt my body heat rising, my pulse quickening. I felt something opening up inside me. This was email, this wasn't supposed to be happening with email. But these feelings were real. She was feeling it too.

More back and forth, hours of email with this new thing between us. *I am liking this mutual seduction we are doing over email,* Catrina wrote. *If only it will work in real life.*

My parents had long gone to bed and I was fighting to keep my eyes open. *So basically you need to get some sleep soon,* wrote Catrina around 2 AM, *and I am leaving for Olympia tomorrow morning, and then we are cut off. Ack! What are we gonna do? You have gotten under my skin and I don't know if I can go without you. Dammit.*

MAP   29

I knew she couldn't afford the long distance bill to call me, and a plane ticket was out of the question. Her whole family was living pretty much paycheck to paycheck. *Being poor has affected my life way more than being a lesbian,* she'd told me a few days before. It felt like so long ago.

We decided to snail mail as much as we could until she got back on email. She sent me her phone number and I promised I'd call as well, sometime that weekend, sometime when my parents would be out of earshot. *I wish you were here,* I wrote.

Call me as much as you want, she wrote back. *We can whisper. You know, I say I love you, but it doesn't seem big enough.*

I love you too, I wrote, *and whatever happens I will always love the you that is coming through my screen tonight, forever.* Finally I went to bed, accompanied by thumpety-thumping heart, Catrina's words over and over, and fear and joy and anticipation scampering every which way. It was hours before I fell asleep.

I woke up around noon and checked email first thing, because Catrina said she would send me one last email before she headed out to her apartment in Olympia. The email was dated early this morning. *I couldn't fall asleep all last night,* she wrote me. *I wanted you here with me so badly it hurt. I've never felt this way about anyone before, I'm scared shitless. I don't know what is going to happen to us, but until we meet, and know for sure, you have my heart.* She added a P.S. *I saw your self-portrait on your web site, I like it, I want to see a picture that shows your face though.*

I felt my insides all queasy in a wonderful new way, and I wanted to email Catrina back immediately except she wouldn't get it until who knew when, months maybe. So I ate as much breakfast as I could keep down and logged on again and started the email to Tyler.

I press *send*. Emailing Tyler about this is not enough. I want to get on the next plane to Washington.

The phone rings as soon as I log off the computer, and my dad picks up and then hollers, *Audrey, it's Matthew!* Mom and Dad are in the next room, so I go down to the basement where there's an old rotary dial phone. I pull the receiver into the little basement room where our extra freezer is kept and I shut the door. I tell Matthew the whole story.

I'm expecting, *you're crazy*. Expecting, *it could be dangerous*. Expecting, *you can't fall in love over email*. I mean, what I'm telling him is the sort of thing usually associated with freaks.

Wow, he says first.

What's she like? he asks. *Where's she from?*

She lives in Olympia, kind of near Seattle. She was an art major, and she just graduated and she's waitressing and trying to figure out what to do with her life. She's thinking about starting a mail-order feminist bookstore.

Cool, Matthew says. *Can you do that without a trust fund?*

I laugh. *I don't know. When I hear her talk about it, I'm glad I'm still in school.*

Do you know what she looks like? Matthew asks next.

I think about how Catrina described herself to me, *light brown hair which I'm growing out, about 135 pounds, I'm not sure, I never bother to weigh myself, why bother, I like what I look like, I have these great breasts, not too small not too large, they're perky, once I pulled my shirt up in a gas station to show them off to my friends.*

I was nervous when Catrina and I wrote each other about how we looked, which was after the falling in love. Would she think I was attractive? What if *she* was really unattractive, the

MAP   31

kind of person people would stare at, repulsed, their eyes asking what I was doing dating her? I wanted to believe it didn't matter but it still did.

Well? Matthew asks, and I realize I haven't answered him yet.

Not exactly, I say. *She sounds cute. She's going to send pictures soon.*

Last week, I tell Matthew, *my mom showed me a newspaper article about a woman who married a man she met in an AOL chat room. The woman figured out four months later that her husband was VERY much not who he'd said he was. My mom knew I'd been emailing people from the Indigo Girls list, so I spent a whole evening trying to explain to her how I knew my list friends weren't axe murderers.*

What did you say?

Well, first I told her that the axe murderers hang out in chat rooms, not on mailing lists about folk singers.

Matthew laughs. *Was she convinced?*

Not exactly. So later I told Catrina that my mom wanted to know if she was an axe murderer, and Catrina wrote back that she'd never murdered an axe in her life.

Matthew laughs again, then says, *technically, she evaded the question. Be careful.*

Do you think it can really work? I ask.

He answers carefully, and as he speaks I start to feel like I'm not the only non-freak this has happened to. *It's not impossible. This woman in my calculus class met a guy over in England through some newsgroup, and they've been together for over a year now. He spent the summer in the States, and she's going to England for spring break.*

Right before I go to sleep, I write Catrina a long letter, *don't be scared, I am too, I love you.* I write with a favorite silver pen on lavender cat stationery left over from summer camp—the only stationery I own—and my slow messy scribbles feel weightier than easy-send, easy-delete, email. These very pages will soon be touched by Catrina's own hands. In the morning I sort through my photos, looking for a few to enclose. I settle on a snapshot someone took of me in Israel and three self-portraits. One self-portrait is a full-body motion photo of me jumping over a bench, and another is the head shot I used for my passport and credit card. The third one is my favorite, partially because my mom had to ask who it was. A side of me I'd somehow managed to keep all to myself. I'm leaning against a patterned tapestry that makes a delicate crown over my head, curve of bra showing, eyes half-closed with a wisp of hair falling onto my face.

I go out and drive Mom's car to the corner store to mail the letter, admiring the stretch of Colonial houses and the snow and ice decorating the trees in my historic suburb-in-the-city neighborhood. It's too stormy to drive around much, so I park the car in the front of the house instead of the alley where it usually goes, lean back in my seat, and listen to *Kind of Blue*. Then I take a deep deep breath and go back into the basement and dial.

Hi, is Catrina there?

It's me.

It's Audrey. My own name sounds funny when I say it, I almost mispronounce it.

Hi.

I'm not sure what to say next, so I ask *how was your drive back to Olympia?*

Her voice is squeaky. High and squeaky. Even though she told

MAP   33

me she had a high squeaky voice, that still throws me. It's not a voice that matches the Catrina I know, catrina@juno.com who's cool and funny and sounds like Tyler in my head.

In my map of this conversation years later there will be gaps. Did I somehow say aloud, *you don't sound like you?* Did she blurt out, *I'm wearing my retainer?* I will remember that we spoke about retainers and extended relatives yet not how we got there or what came next or even whether Catrina wore a retainer. I will remember wondering if we had exhausted all the important topics over email, if it would be *my retainer smells weird* and *did you buy dog food* from here on out. I will remember talking and listening and talking and listening, and my mind, somewhere above and detached from it all, spinning, spinning.

I breathe the damp basement air and curl the white cord of the telephone around my arm and stare at the brightly-lit lists taped to the freezer: 4 ice cream, 1 blintzes, 3 chicken breasts, 3 lentil soup, and so on, and I listen to Catrina's voice. Am I really in love with her, with a person who sounds like this, is having this particular conversation? She hasn't mentioned the fact that we're supposed to be in love. She's not saying *I love you.* Where is the Catrina I know from email? Did I make a mistake?

I think we're both afraid to end the conversation. There's an awkward pause, and then another, and I get the sense that if I don't say the words now, this will be it. *I love you.*

I love you too.

Somehow it's not how I expected those words to sound. It's like the meaning is separate, like we're acting, like we're not sure if we believe what we're saying. I wanted it to sound passionate and hot and intense. But then Catrina asks, *when are you coming to Washington?*

She says it like she wants me to come now, like this is serious and what are we waiting for.

I start to speak and then pause, wishing she was the one with the money for the plane ticket. *I don't know,* I say. When she doesn't say anything else, I say, *the summer I guess.*

That far away?

She wants me to come earlier, and I'm scared.

After we hang up, I look at my watch and realize we were on the phone for close to two hours. I go back and reread all her emails, which still don't jive with Catrina-on-the-phone. *What the hell am I doing?* I ask myself. *How many times have I made fun of other people who did this sort of thing?* But as I'm going through the emails, I start to get the old feeling back, the feeling from before the phone call. I reach the last email I sent Catrina: *I don't take enough risks in my life, so I will see this one through.*

Definitely Something Going On

The snowstorm has let up a little, but not much, and I announce to my surprised parents that I am going outside to shovel. The snow is coming down in big wet globs. I'm in long johns and jeans, layered shirts, a heavy winter coat. My feet are warm in my waterproof boots. If not for the bright red earmuffs—a discount store purchase—I could be a walking advertisement for L.L. Bean. I fumble through my gloves to pull my scarf over the one remaining patch of exposed skin and grasp a shovel. I've got all this pent-up energy, questions without answers and a need to be outdoors, to feel connected with something grounded and larger than I can possibly be.

When I was a little kid, there was a blizzard, and we have photographs of me helpfully trudging through waist-deep snow to clear a path for my father's shovel. My father pulled me to the corner store in my red plastic sled so we could buy milk, exchanging pleasantries with neighbors we rarely spoke to in good weather. In later years, Dad would pay me two dollars to do my part of the shoveling. I was responsible for a few stretches of sidewalk and a flight of stairs, while he shoveled the driveway and the rest of the stairs. When the snow was this heavy, I'd grumble and try to get him to raise my pay to two-fifty. Now, shoveling the short stretch of pavement by the back door where I learned to ride a tricycle, I am wondering, *what next?*

What if I just never call Catrina again? Soon she would be a vague memory, a novel I never finished reading. I'd leave the Indigo Girls list and make the most of my last semester at Penn and move to Boston after graduation and wonder if any of this really happened. If it meant anything.

The snow lands on my glasses, my coat, the sidewalk I've already cleared. I lift a shovelful, then another. I can hear my breath.

I have this new image of Catrina from the conversation, nervous and timid, not at all what I pictured or how she described herself. So different from the Catrina whose last email read *until we meet, and know for sure, you have my heart.* Is it just her voice? Is Catrina a different person over email? How can I fuse the separate images in my brain, email and telephone voice and the photos she's sending me and finally the real live person?

Shoveling exhausts me fairly quickly. I am back to my childhood, ready to whine to my father, but he is inside and I am the one who chose this. I am determined not to give up. I clear snow from a few more feet of sidewalk, reaching the edge of this stretch. My arms are tired, will be sore tomorrow, but that doesn't mean I have to go inside. I rest the shovel against the house, climb the unshoveled steps up the hill, and head down the semi-plowed alley as I have countless times before.

The familiarity of my surroundings clashes with the foreign ground in my head. I've never been here before. I am in a country I never learned about in school, a land that never appeared in my storybooks, a place where my family has never traveled. I am in uncharted territory, and I wish for a map.

Turning up Cooke Street, I notice a funny sign in the corner

MAP   37

store window, *Pink and White Lightbulbs 4 SALE,* and there's no one around to laugh with me. I want to tell someone but Catrina's the only one who sees the humor in lightbulbs, and in my head Catrina is an email address arriving on a computer screen *you have new mail.*

Back home I go into the basement to use the phone again. I'll just tell Catrina quickly about the lightbulb sign, five minutes and then hang up, maybe leave a message on her machine, but she's home and we end up talking for an hour. We talk about which Indigo Girls bootlegs we want most, and then the best vacations we've been on—hers hiking in Utah, mine a toss-up between a family trip to Israel and a spring break in Cyprus—and then we brainstorm ideas for her bookstore business, our ideas feeding off each other as Catrina hunts for paper to scribble them down. It's not at all the intensity of our emails but I feel like I'm talking to a good friend, and this time when I say *I love you* at the end, it doesn't sound like a non sequitur, it sounds comfortable.

In time I'll realize that all of us are different over email, even me. It's inevitable. We are given both time and space to respond, in a medium that provides the illusion of immediacy and a whole new form of intimacy. We can be braver or more thoughtful or kinder. We can be mean and cruel without the usual consequence. We can disappear, we can open up, we can wear a personality we're too shy to wear in public. And even if we choose none of these options consciously, the mere existence of the choice impacts how we present ourselves and how we are received.

I'm working part-time this vacation, and on Monday I listen to AJ's mix as I drive in to work. It's the same drive as last week and the ordinariness strikes me, how all this can be going on while Mom and Dad and the people who see me every day at work don't have any idea. There aren't dates or flowers or overheard knocks at bedroom windows providing clues. I stuff envelopes and joke with coworkers and hug parents and the whole time the vibrancy inside me is hidden away like the secrets of a closed book.

The last time I kept something this big from my parents was in high school when I decided not to tell them I had made it into the *Cum Laude* Society until a couple of days before the assembly. Success in my family was always measured against the one hundred percent mark, *expected,* but I hadn't expected *Cum Laude* and I wanted my whole family to be surprised and savor the achievement with me. Instead of the reaction I'd anticipated from them, I received anger. *We pay for your tuition, we deserve to know.*

I just told you.

No. That's not good enough. You knew two weeks ago.

Audrey, said my father, *if you ever try to pull this in college we will stop paying your tuition.*

I looked to Mom, but this was a solid front of more parental fury than I had ever seen. I tried to explain and was met with, *what do you mean, you were surprised? We're not surprised. You're one of the smartest people in that school.*

When it comes to relationships, I'm caught between my parents' unspoken conflicted messages: *no one is good enough for our daughter* and *what's wrong with her or us or how we raised her that our daughter hasn't had a boyfriend since age twelve.* I think my dad prefers to keep his daddy's-little-girl image of me, while my mom wants to believe that I have more experience than I'm

MAP   39

telling them. Thanks to Mom's interrogative style and my lim-
ited experience, the truth is she knows just about everything.

Mom has a talent for asking detailed questions I don't want
to answer but can never evade. Robbing me of the feeling of it
being *my* experience in the process. She's so good at it that now
she doesn't even have to say anything—I can *sense* her response.
If she knew about Catrina it would be *are you sure you're not
interpreting her wrong* and *why can't she make half the phone
calls* and *I don't think you should be spending so much money to fly
out there during the school year* and *if you do get married won't it
bother you that she's not Jewish* and *it's not safe to stay with someone you've never met without having a backup plan.* The truth is
some of those questions are in the back of my mind somewhere
now. I just don't want to think about them yet. I want to give
myself time to see where this unexpected relationship is going,
to fully experience the journey.

I call Catrina on Monday night and again on Wednesday after
my parents go to sleep. Our conversations are gaining a rhythm,
a good one. I don't notice when it happens, but somewhere in
there I stop doubting this is real and go back to hoping it will
last, hoping it will work in person.

They have sublets by the university which are pretty cheap,
Catrina tells me on Wednesday. I think about finding a web job
in Seattle for the summer, or maybe just taking a month or two
off to write and hang out there with Catrina.

I talk to Tyler on Thursday. Tyler hasn't decided if she's bi or
gay or what, but she tells me that there's definitely something
going on between her and Heather, it started during finals. I say

I thought Heather was straight. *Nope, she's gay,* Tyler says confidently. *Don't tell anyone about us though,* Tyler says. *I mean, not like you see my Penn friends, but don't tell anyone from the list either.*

I won't, I promise. *Have you told anyone else?* I ask.

Just my friend Kelly, she says. *She's my one friend who's not from my hometown or Penn. One of my high school friends just joined the Brown les-bi-gay group, so I might tell her too, but some of my other high school friends might not be cool with it and I don't want it to get around.*

I feel a sudden protectiveness of Tyler. Although part of me is jealous that she's reached this point of self-knowledge so much sooner than I did, I don't envy the social situation it puts her in. I remember how important my high school friends were during my first year of college, before I'd built a decent Penn support system, and how hard it has always been to be different from everyone else in a new environment.

Oh, Tyler says, before I can say anything. *This is random. You know Jordanna from the list? Heather found out the other day that Jordanna had seen pictures from that list party in Seattle a few months ago, and she was asking Jordanna about what everyone looked like. Anyway, I was curious too so Heather forwarded me Jordanna's email, and Jordanna mentioned that Catrina was cute.*

I'd like to believe that I don't care what other people think, but even hours later this third-party assessment of Catrina's attractiveness makes me feel good.

On Friday afternoon I hang out with my best friend Sasha, listening to some of her poetry in the incense-filled bedroom with deep salmon walls she painted during middle school. As Sasha reads, I flip through pictures of her school friends, trying to get a feel for the parts of her life I don't see. Sasha's not the kind of

MAP   41

best friend you talk to all the time, she's more like a sister. We met when we were babies, and our families went to the same synagogue and got together all the time when we were growing up. Even though it's hard to imagine life without Sasha, she's attending art school in Oregon and sometimes months will go by now when we don't see or talk to each other.

I have no idea who these people are, captured goofy and serious in four-by-six, what they mean to Sasha. I flip past more blurry smiles and reach a shot of two people kissing. I have to look twice to be certain—yes, the photo I'm holding shows Sasha kissing a girl.

Last fall when Sasha mentioned going to a meeting of the lesbian gay bisexual association at her school, I asked her *are you bi?* She had said to me then, *I think everybody is,* but I didn't know exactly how to take it. She'd already had two long-term boyfriends. Did she like women or just the idea? Wasn't it just not cool to be straight in art school?

Now I can't stop staring at this photo. It's sexy and playful and I'm happy Sasha's eyes are on the page and not on my envious ones. I want to be as comfortable with someone, as sexy and playful in my touch, as what I see here.

When Sasha finishes her poem, I ask who the girl is and Sasha tells me it's a friend of hers. I still hesitate to mention Catrina, since Sasha's not an email person and could easily think I'm a freak, but finally I open up. *Congratulations,* Sasha says, giving me a hug. *I'm glad you found someone.*

I remember the day I said to Matthew *I want a girlfriend.* I'd called Sasha after that. She was telling me about a guy she was kind of seeing and another guy she was attracted to and a third guy she was going to go camping with that winter, and then I said *I want a girlfriend* and Sasha said *me too.* And then I asked *will you go out with me?* as she asked *will you marry me?* and we laughed together and it was so perfect and I knew she knew I just meant it like I wanted one in that moment.

Later, as we're downstairs eating pita with her mom's home-made hummus, Sasha says *ask me if I'm a tree.* I say *are you a tree?* and Sasha says *no* and then Sasha says *ask me if I'm a heli-copter.* I ask *are you a helicopter?* like I'm supposed to and Sasha says *do I look like a helicopter?* in that Sasha way of hers. It's an old and stupid joke but that's the kind that Sasha likes to tell. We're laughing hysterically and I want to stay but it's getting late, almost sundown, and I promised to be home for Shabbat dinner, so I call home and say I'm leaving in about fifteen min-utes. Sasha walks me out to the car and says I should come visit her in Oregon this spring, and I think, *Oregon and Washington are next-door neighbors.*

Driving back, I sing to myself, cheesy love songs of my adoles-cence that are finally starting to make sense. As I pull into the driveway, I can see the glow of our house through the windows. I forego the stairs and run down the hill in three steps, a fourth step up to the back porch, and unlock the door. *Hello?* I shout up, the usual *I'm-home-who-else-is* family greeting, and hear my parents' two *hellos* in return.

Three places are set and the smell of my father's fresh-baked *challah* permeates the kitchen. Candles are set in the candle-sticks Sasha's grandmother gave me for my Bat Mitzvah, a tray underneath to catch the drips. As my parents come downstairs, I open the door to the front porch and look out at the deep pink and blue sky.

Sunset alert! I say, our family catch-phrase for a particularly beautiful sunset. I'm especially glad of the rituals tonight,

MAP   43

because they help to hide that I've been avoiding talking to my parents. The three of us pause and watch the sunset, and then the timer goes off and Mom goes to check on the soup. Dad and I follow her into the kitchen.

Mom lights the candles, and I cover my eyes and peek through my fingers at the flicker as I race to finish the silent blessing faster than her. *Good Shabbos,* we each say at the end, and take turns hugging and kissing, me feeling awkward while Mom and Dad share a few-second long kiss. Dad puts his hand on my head and blesses me in Hebrew and English, *may God make you like Sarah and Rebecca, Rachel and Leah, bless and protect you....and grant you peace,* and then as Dad and I sing *ki hu yom techilah* off-key, Mom sways her wine glass, conductor-style. I uncover the raisin-filled *challah,* making everyone admire before cutting the end piece for Dad, middle piece for Mom, last for me.

I recite the *motzi,* the blessing over bread. Mom asks about my day, and I try to guess what ingredients she used in the dinner. Dad listens. After we finish eating, we wave our hands to make the dishes go away, which never works but we keep trying anyway.

I wonder as I scrape plates and wipe the table how to tell them what's going on. Mom will flip out about it being email. Dad should get the email part, since he's had email buddies for years—they were trying to create a global Jewish network, before the days of the web—but the love thing is definitely a wild card. It's not coming out to Dad, exactly, that I'm nervous about. It's breaking the news that daddy's little girl thinks about things like love and sex.

Once the dishes are taken care of, I join Mom in my parents' bedroom, and Dad goes into the den as usual to play on the computer. *It's not playing,* my dad insists. He says he gets work done. My parents have the same job title, *College Professor,* but Dad seems to have a lot more fun. He teaches math, which is like breathing for him. Mom is only relaxing with a Toni Morrison book tonight because she's spent her entire day cooking and freezing meals for the next semester. She teaches marketing and fashion merchandising, and she'll probably wake up early tomorrow to start preparing lectures.

Mom asks me to close the bedroom door since Dad has on a different station in the other room. *I don't need to hear two competing televisions,* she says. Neither of them actually watch television, just leave it on as background. Tonight's *Wonder Years* rerun is the one with Kevin and Winnie's first kiss, so I don't even pretend to be working on my paper. I used to have a huge crush on Kevin. Now he looks so *young.* I'm nearly done with college and he's just beginning junior high. But he's got it easy, he's kissing Winnie who his parents already know and love, while I'm just imagining kissing Catrina and breaking the news.

Catrina isn't out to her parents either. She wants to tell them. *There's all this family shit going on right now,* she says, *it's too complicated to explain, I'll tell you when you're out here. I think being a lesbian is the greatest thing and I wish I knew they would agree. I don't know what they'll say. My little sister knows and I think it's making her more tolerant.*

I look at Mom, who is engrossed in her book, dressed for bed with a turtleneck under her nightgown. I don't want to do the big speech thing and start off with *Mom, Dad, I'm bi.* I kind of want to wait until I visit Catrina to say anything, wait until I'm in Washington lying in Catrina's bed and she's got her arms around me kissing me and trying to be quiet while I say into the phone, *guess what? Catrina and I are seeing each other...* It doesn't seem as simple as when I wrote home *I have a boyfriend* from

MAP   45

summer camp after sixth grade, but I always promised myself if I was serious about someone I would tell my parents.

As the credits roll on *Wonder Years*, Mom decides she wants ice cream.

What kind do we have? I ask.

Breyer's, she says, *vanilla bean and chocolate.*

Breyer's vanilla bean is my favorite ice cream, and there's a coffee can of Mom's homemade Polish tea cookies in the freezer, which would make an excellent ice cream sandwich. I'm salivating just thinking about it. I'm also very comfortable, curled under the covers because our house goes down to fifty-five degrees at night. Dad is convinced that fifty-five degrees is warm. Why Mom and I think eating ice cream is going to make us warmer, I don't know, but that's my family.

It's understood that Mom isn't going to be the one to get the ice cream. Once she goes upstairs after dinner, she's up for the night. *Let Daddy get it,* I say.

You're not helpless, Mom says.

I stick out my tongue, say *watch this,* and pick up the phone next to my dad's side of the bed. We have two phone lines because Dad spends so much time on the modem. The light for line two isn't lit up so I know he's not online. I use the second line to dial our main phone number.

He picks up on the second ring. *Hello?*

Hi, Daddy. It's your favorite daughter. I use my cutest voice. *Are you getting a lot of work done?*

Yes, he says.

Good, I say.

Then he says, *At least I was until I got interrupted by my favorite daughter.*

Well, since you've already been interrupted, I suggest helpfully, *don't you think it's time for a break? Mommy and I were thinking about ice cream.*

My mom shakes her head at me, but she can't hide her smirk. I give her my most innocent little-girl smile.

We have some ice cream in the freezer, my dad says. *And while you're at it, you could bring me a scoop.*

Oh. I say. *I thought you would get it for us. Because you're my best dad, and I'm only home for a little while.*

He hesitates.

Please? I say. *It's scary downstairs at night.*

Okay, he agrees. *Let me finish making up this algebra problem for my 101 class, and then I'll bring us all ice cream.*

Thanks, Daddy, I say. I hang up and grin at my mom, who's biting her hand so she won't laugh. *See, he's bringing us ice cream.*

She gives up and laughs.

Ode to Catrina

It's the next afternoon and I've dragged my Powerbook and an afghan and a stack of books and notes downstairs to the living room where it's quiet and separate from the rest of the house. I'm trying to trick myself into getting work done. The living room is for company, and growing up I wasn't allowed to bring my friends inside. Instead, they'd peer through the glass-paned doors at the Oriental rug, the antique sewing machines, the shofar from Israel over the fireplace, the red velvet couch. The doors are kept closed in the winter to keep the cold from entering the rest of the house, and there's not a phone jack nearby, no temptations.

I curl up in the afghan on the couch and open the file on my Powerbook called *History Paper* along with a new one I call *Ode to Catrina*. I'm hoping that if I leave the *Ode to Catrina* file in the background and add bits to it as they enter my head, there will be space for history paper thoughts to come through, instead of just snippets of a letter I want to write to the woman I love. It sounds so wonderful, *the woman I love*. Odd how you can be alone for so long, then suddenly so wonderfully happy and intertwined with someone else.

I am settling into the idea that this will work, that it isn't just a temporary electronic fantasy. Pictures came today. How can I explain in words the first glimpse of each photo, and the accompanying knowledge that I will make love to this woman someday? Should I say make love *to* or *with*, perhaps both. The one is more ferocious and the other tender. Just thinking about it I want her here now, on my lap where this Powerbook sits, kissing me and brushing the paper aside until later. If she were here, could I concentrate, her fingers on top of mine as I try to type?

I can't concentrate anyway. I open the envelope with her handwriting again, pausing as I notice how she wrote my name, the difference between her handwriting and her email style. She would look different in a picture of her writing to me, I think. There's not a picture showing that introspective joy. My favorite photo shows her with her head in her hand, hood pulled up on her purple sweatshirt. *This was from my summer of despair,* Catrina wrote on the back. She looks vulnerable enough that I would be welcome, my arms around her, maybe my lips to her forehead. But not hopeless--this is someone you would *want* to comfort, not someone you would run from for fear of being dragged down too deep. Someone who would also be able to *give* that comfort. The rest of the photos are more public, making faces at the camera, jumping on a trampoline, hiking in the desert. She comes across in those as someone who isn't afraid to take risks, who definitely has her own style, who is going to keep you laughing but still has depth. I can tell from those photos that we'll be friends and soulmates forever even if as lovers it doesn't work out. She's got her shit together in them, almost even too cool for me, I can't see the space for intimacy. It's there, though, I know it. That's the photo I would take. Catrina full of confidence and fears and me.

MAP 49

My camp counselor in Israel, Cory, said once that he thought there were maybe twenty-five people for each person. I think that's true. Finding them is hard, some people find none and a few find two or three. There has to be more than one potential soulmate out there, or else chaos theory could be the end of happiness. So many odds against you finding each other at the right place and right time. Thank you snowstorm for trapping Catrina in a place where she had access to email, thank you Indigo Girls mailing list, thank you email addiction.

On the dorm newsgroup, my friend Miguel wanted to know how to tell if you are in love. I said when you are willing to have a kid and a dog and move to Washington for her. He wanted to know whether he was moving or I was, so I said he could come along, we'd need neighbors.

How else to tell? When your imagined lotto winnings are going to pay off her college loans and you can feel the spaces along your body where she belongs. When after she asks if you're allergic to down pillows there's a long pause in the conversation and you both know what would be happening during that pause if it weren't for the land between the coasts. When you want to describe to her exactly what you'd be doing to her and she'd be doing to you as you watch *The Sound of Music* together, but you're afraid to jinx it by being explicit—what if your bodies have something different and better in mind and you're still caught in a spoken fantasy—so instead you just start wishing away states, one by one, and hope she understands how much you want her.

I wonder about the future, about that first meeting. In the airport, will we hug, kiss, make out, will I start to fall over losing my balance from the weight of the backpack? I'll watch her as she drives, I relish that, hope I don't make her nervous enough that we're in an accident. What time of day will it be, I wonder? I don't think I'll bother bringing a sleeping bag, but what if it's awkward for awhile? We'll need to plan to use the beginning time to adjust, it would be hard to roll into bed with someone before you've watched her walk around, before you've focused on her hand holding a coffee mug or the shape of her upper lip when she smiles. What if I'm just tired? Long plane ride, no sleep the night before from anticipation, then jetlag, at nine I'll be ready to fall asleep and she'll be just warming up.

Should I even be imagining this far? Intentions can change, we might just spend the days and nights hanging out, can you really plan to have sex with someone before meeting in person? It's all absurd in a way, but in another way it's not at all. I want to lay down and talk awhile, fall asleep in each other's arms then wake up in the morning, learn each other's bodies slowly, quietly, and her eyes, her eyes...how close do we have to be with my glasses off for her eyes to be in focus?

Under the Covers

It's one AM my time, ten PM hers. Lights are off, phone pulled up to my bed. I'm curled under the covers because it's fifty-five degrees in the house, and I'm whispering so I don't wake my parents in the next room.

I wish you lived closer.

I do too.

I want you.

There's the kind of pause that, if we were in person, would be filled by touch. In my head there's a map of the continent, Catrina at the far left, by the Pacific Ocean, me here at the right-most edge, cords and poles and telephone wires spanning the distance.

How long would it take to walk?

Too long.

Maybe I can visit over spring break, I say. Two months away instead of four.

I'd like that, Catrina says. She's whispering too—her roommate is around. *I wish I had enough money to fly to Philly. Then we could see each other next week.*

The part of me between my legs wants to buy her a ticket right now.

I visited the bank today, Catrina says. *To see about getting a loan,* to start my mail-order bookstore business. She tells me about the different loan options, about the tellers at Seafirst who know her by name. She loves her local bank. It's not some huge conglomerate and that appeals to her values. It appeals to mine too, but mostly I just like the name. Seafirst. It sounds coastal. *There's a lot of paperwork to fill out,* she continues. *And they want to see a business plan, so I need to write one.*

Have you come up with a name for your business yet? I ask.

No, she says. *It's not as easy as naming Zoe.*

But Zoe isn't even conceived yet, I tease.

I know, she says. *I'm doing the business because I have to support myself, but I really just want to be a mom. Your writing can support us after Zoe comes, right? Hey, did I ever tell you I saw my little sister being born?*

Really? I say. *Weren't you only five years old then?*

Yeah. My mom did a natural childbirth, right in the living room, and we all watched. Except my brother, because he fell asleep. I was the first person to hold her, after my mom.

That's so neat. I think about what I know about my own birth. It was in a big hospital, and my dad was there helping my mom remember her Lamaze breathing, which must have hurt because of her ribs. *Did I tell you how I broke two of my mom's ribs when she was pregnant with me?*

Wow.

Yeah, she was seven months pregnant, and I guess I kicked too hard or something. They couldn't do anything, she just had to go around in pain until my birthday. Every so often she'll mention it and I'll apologize all over again.

I hope Zoe doesn't do that to me.

She won't, I promise, like it's in my power to arrange. *I'll be right back, I have to go to the bathroom.*

MAP 53

Okay, I'm going to brush my teeth while you do that.

I rest the receiver next to my Pooh bear and tiptoe down the hall to the bathroom. The night light is on, so I don't turn on any other lights. I try to wash my hands quietly, and then look at myself in the dark glow of a mirror for a long moment. This is really me, here, now.

I tiptoe back to my room, kiss Pooh's forehead, and put the receiver up to my ear again. *Are you back?*

Yeah. My mouth is all sparkly-feeling. What kind of toothpaste do you use?

Crest, I say. *Or Colgate. Sometimes Aqua Fresh.*

You should try Tom's of Maine, Catrina says. *It's all natural.*

Is it approved by the American Dental Association? I ask.

I don't know. She offers to look, but I say I'd rather talk to her than wait for her to read the back of her toothpaste, so she says she'll check later, after I go to sleep, and then says, *What if I have a boy? I don't think I could deal with a boy. I'm counting on having Zoe. Would my lesbian feminist body really give me a boy?*

I'd help you with a boy, I say. *I used to babysit boys, and they were fun. Except for the time they got into the knives. But we're not having knives in our house anyway, because me and knives don't get along. Have I shown you my scars?*

No, let me see. I'll kiss them.

I point to the V-shaped scar on the middle finger of my left hand as though she's not three thousand miles away. *See, that's from my dad's challah knife, from fifth grade.*

Catrina blows a kiss through the phone wires and promises to kiss it for real when I come west. We talk for a while longer, but soon my eyes are beginning to shut and I'm yawning every other sentence. Catrina will be out late with friends tomorrow evening, so we make plans to talk the night after that.

I love you, Catrina says.

I love you too.

Dream of me.

Okay, you too.

Okay, good night.

Good night. I rest the receiver in its cradle, pull Pooh into the nook of my arm, and fall asleep thinking Catrina-thoughts.

Why Don't You Just Call Yourself a Lesbian?

Aren't you a little nervous about the email thing? AJ asks me, flicking some ash into a crushed soda can, her makeshift ash-tray. We're sitting in the back of Chats on her break, so she can smoke. *What if she's not who she says she is?*

I can tell, I say. It's probably the most common question I've been asked since returning from winter break, but generally people seem curious, not shocked. Everyone seems to have a story of someone who something like this has happened to. I tell AJ, *the kind of things we talk about, the details, you can't make up. In some ways I know her better than my closest friends.*

In time I will think about AJ's question differently. *What if she's not who she says she is?* is a question for any person, any relationship, not just those begun via the internet. Humans, no matter how well-intentioned, are flawed. People have secrets. White lies darken. You can believe, you can trust, you can learn a lot about someone, but you can never know if *anyone* is being one hundred percent truthful about everything. Yet inventing a character as richly nuanced as a real live human being, and sustaining that deception over an extended period of time—even with the help of email and the absence of in-person interaction—requires a skillset akin to that of a master novelist. The less masterful usually slip up, the way nearly all of us slip up when trying to sustain a lie. I am wrong in my answer to AJ—you *can* make up details—but it's hard, incredibly hard, to *invent* the juxtaposition and specificity and complexity and randomness of detail after detail that comes naturally in our everyday interaction and that we recognize, both instinctively and under inspection, as truth.

AJ's holding the cigarette away from me so I'm not getting direct whiffs, but the whole area smells like smoke and it's kind of gross. *I know it's a bad habit,* she says. *I quit for a while, but over vacation I was hanging out with friends who smoke and got back in the habit.* I'm allergic, and I used to refuse to be friends with people who smoke, but it's gotten harder. Now I mostly just ask them to blow away from me.

Let me know if you want me to confiscate the pack, I say.

No thanks, she says. *Maybe when I get back from Australia. I hear they smoke a lot over there.* AJ's studying abroad this spring, but her semester doesn't start until late March. *Oh, did I tell you I broke it off completely with the Vermont guy?*

AJ tells me about the breakup, then reports that she has dates with three different guys this weekend. *Don't think I'm usually like this,* AJ says. *It just happened.*

I laugh, taking off my faded green baseball cap, pushing my hair out of the way, and then putting the cap on backwards. AJ watches me do this, and then asks, *do you ever wear makeup?*

I tried it once in eighth grade at a party, I say. *I haven't worn it since.*

Why not? AJ asks.

Because my mom saw me and she liked it, I say. I'm kidding, mostly. My mom *did* like it, which surprised me—I had expected her to get mad—but the real reason is that I *didn't* like wearing

MAP   57

makeup very much. It took me out of my comfort zone and didn't feel like me, and it didn't bring about a magical transformation that might have made it worthwhile.

The occasion was a makeover party at Gretchen Forrester's. Dana Nichols was in charge of my makeover, but she kept consulting with the other girls. I agreed easily to nailpolish, which I'd played with at home. They wanted to do something to my eyes, mascara and something else I don't remember the name of, but I didn't want anything to get into my eyes by mistake. Maybe I told them I'd get in trouble, or they realized I wasn't going to take my glasses off so it was pointless, or maybe I was simply adamant enough about it that they gave up.

One of the other girls suggested doing something to my hair, something involving curlers, *please, it would look so cute, I do it to my sister's hair all the time.* I hesitated. *You can wash it right out.* I imagined my parents' reaction, the raised eyebrows and held-back comments meaning *why were you doing something so stupid?*

Dana chimed in, *it really would look great on you,* as the doorbell rang and someone peeked out the window to see Parker and Vince on the front steps. There might have been a squeal or two—almost every girl in the eighth grade had a crush on one or the other. Gretchen ran down to greet the two boys and make sure they didn't come upstairs.

Most of the room emptied out as the girls took turns standing over the stairwell and shouting down at the boys. My nails were drying, so I wasn't allowed to move, and I didn't know how to shout to two boys who were cooler than I was.

What do you say, Audge? Dana asked, when the ruckus had died down.

The other girls were urging me on. And it wasn't permanent. And Parker and Vince were downstairs and I guess in a way I thought maybe this was my chance.

Someone crimped my hair with the curling iron and Dana put lipstick on me—pink to match my favorite hot pink sweater— and then waved a hairdryer over my frosted pink nails and pronounced them dry. I remember thinking, would the boys be interested in me now? But even though they said *whoa, Auuuuuudge,* and maybe whistled as I came downstairs, I knew it was for the other girls' sake. It didn't change anything. Simply the way they said my name proved they were still cooler than me and left me tongue-tied.

It took so much time, I tell AJ, after describing the makeover party. *I was bored. It wasn't fun. It definitely wasn't me. And makeup costs money and I had better things to spend my money on. Like books.*

I never really thought about the money part of it, AJ says. Her forehead wrinkles like she's doing the mental calculations.

But it's more than that though, I say. *There's something stupid about the whole concept. You're wasting all this money and time to try to get the attention of people who would ignore you other- wise.* What I can't quite articulate is that makeup, worn for this purpose, becomes a kind of closet, and in doing so covers the person inside with a coat of insecurity. *I'd rather focus on people who like me for who I am.*

AJ hears me. She tells me she doesn't think about makeup for herself that way. She talks about how she enjoys wearing it, about how it makes *her* feel. I can't decide if I believe her, or if I think she's bought into the myth. But I like that she's listening to me. I like that we're having the conversation.

MAP   59

Then she says she wants to see me totally made up.

I tell her it's never going to happen.

Just once? she begs, stubbing the cigarette. *Before I leave for Australia?*

I shake my head.

I shave under my arms, Catrina says. *But not my legs. The hair is light so you can't really tell anyway.*

I shave my legs, I say. *But not very often in the winter, because no one can see it unless I'm going to synagogue and have to wear a skirt, so it doesn't matter. I hate shaving—it's almost as time-con- suming as makeup. It gets scratchy, though.*

Is your leg hair brown like the hair on your head? Catrina asks.

Mmhm, I say, wondering if I'll like the feel of Catrina's hairy legs. I make a mental note to shave the night before and pack a razor when I finally visit.

Is all your *hair that color?* she asks.

It takes a moment for me to realize what she's asking. *Yeah,* I say, too shy all of a sudden to ask her the question back.

Catrina and I are talking at least once a day now. When I hear her squeaky *hi, it's me* on the machine I get butterflies inside. My body is responding in ways it always has to physical attraction, the way it did when I was fourteen listening to my Tom Cruise look-alike counselor play guitar, the way it did when I was sev- enteen and my History teacher passed me unexpectedly in the hall and asked, *how's it going,* the way it did when I watched the sex scene in *Go Fish.* And yet it's different, too, not because we haven't met in person, but because of the love part.

That weekend I go to a party with friends from my dorm.

The crowd is mixed, drinkers and non-drinkers, and I'm holding a mix of 7-Up and peach schnapps with no intentions of getting drunk. Catrina's on my mind, and I know that when I leave, I'll call and talk to her for at least an hour. It's strange to have a girlfriend and yet be spending my Saturday night alone, not being with her, even though *being with her* right now consists of hours alone in my apartment on the phone. I feel different, being here, than I have at other parties. I'm not looking around fantasizing. I don't really care that the random guy my friend and I have been talking to is by any standards fairly hot.

Music and dim lights and the ambiance of alcohol give me this vague sense of being buzzed. *If you two break up,* Random Guy asks, *would you go back to guys?* It seems like such a theoretical question.

I can't even envision that, I say. *I truly see my future with Catrina.*

Ever since getting back from winter vacation, I've been talking about my girlfriend all over the place—because I can, because I finally have someone to talk about, because I'm in love, because I can't keep it in. I'm OUT now, in big capital letters. And it's no big deal. A couple of straight male friends who saw the pictures admired my taste, and I felt a sense of male connection that had previously eluded me. Other than that, telling people has been uneventful. I wonder if maybe my friends are more liberal than most. Or maybe it's just how casually you bring up the subject, how confident you are. I'm sure it's a lot more comfortable to be around someone who's glowing as they say *I'm in love, her name is...* than someone stammering, *I think I have, uh, these feelings for, uh, women.*

Why don't you just call yourself a lesbian? Random Guy wants

MAP   61

to know. The answer seems so obvious. *Because I'm not.* But he presses further and that's when the answer really becomes clear. It's more than simply the attraction to guys which has always been there, and more than the attraction to women that I'm just beginning to explore. It's about potential, about possibility, about open-mindedness, and especially about making choices based on values and individuals rather than mere gender.

A few years later, when I haven't been drawn to men in a while, I'll start using the word queer to describe myself. I'll choose *queer* because *queer* will fit me better than either *bisexual* or *lesbian,* because *queer* places less emphasis on sex and more on overall identity, because it carries a connotation of confidence and empowerment, because there is space for fluidity inside, because it encompasses a larger community, because it won't be such a scary radical word to me anymore, because it is one bold and easy syllable.

My friend has wandered off. Random Guy has gone from talking about his second cousin who met someone online in a chatroom to describing the details of a toast he gave at someone's bachelor party. He's trying to remember the words, gives up, starts in on his philosophy of giving speeches and how you're supposed to wear an outrageous tie so everyone remembers your tie and doesn't notice if you mess up your speech. I've lost interest a while ago but he's still rambling on, oblivious, my identity invisible to him in some fundamental way.

I'm looking for a way out of this conversation, waiting for the break where I can excuse myself to go to the bathroom. Two more guys come over, *did you hear what happened on the news?* and I shake my head and Random Guy says *yeah, that blows, I'm getting a refill* and he's gone, and now I'm faking my way through some discussion I never wanted to be part of in the first place. It takes finishing my 7-Up and gesturing towards the punch bowl to maneuver an exit. I think about how easy it is to connect with Catrina, and for the first time, I wonder if maybe it isn't my flaw after all, this gap I now think I've always felt with guys, not knowing how to be in relation to them.

An hour later I'm back on the phone with Catrina. *Have I mentioned lately how much I love you?*

Tell me again, she says. *I had a rotten day at work and I've been going through Audrey-withdrawal for the last few hours.*

I love you, I say. *And you'll be leaving that job really really soon.* I conjure up my mental picture of the cafe where she's supposed to start working in a week or two. I picture sunlight and hand-painted mugs and colorful walls and people with dreadlocks.

I'm counting the days, she says, sighing.

I think I'm going to pledge a sorority, Tyler announces to me the next morning.

I thought you were just rushing because you were curious, I say.

I met a bunch of really cool people at last night's mixer, Tyler says. *I think it might be fun.*

She sounds sincere. She doesn't sound like she's been brainwashed. She sounds like the same friend who a week ago was joking with me about *this rush bullshit.*

If she pledges, I'm sure she'll get in.

I'm envious of Tyler's ability to fit in, to be someone who can get picked by a sorority if she wants to be. I never even rushed. The concept brought me back to elementary school, to gym class, to school dances. There are some places where the

MAP   63

lines of coolness and acceptance blur, and others where there is no murky space. Sororities don't have murky space—to express your interest in joining one is to give someone else the power to exclude you.

Did you wind up going to that party last night? Tyler asks. *How was it?*

I tell her about the conversation with Random Guy.

It's cool that you can tell people about Catrina, Tyler says. *I kind of want to tell my friends about Heather, but I don't know what to come out as.*

Take your time, I advise her. *Especially if you think you might pledge—feel it out first. What do you think you are?*

I don't know, she says. *Happy.* She hasn't decided on a label, and says she'd rather just enjoy the relationship than try to figure it out. I'm awed by her ability to do that, impressed that she can be at peace with the uncertainty. *Heather wishes I were a lesbian,* Tyler tells me. *She basically thinks I am one and just don't realize it yet.*

Why? I ask.

I guess she doesn't want me to leave her for a guy.

That's dumb, I say. *I mean, if someone leaves you, does it really matter who they leave you for? If the relationship was working, it wouldn't have happened in the first place.*

Exactly, says Tyler. *Catrina's a lesbian, right? How does she feel about you being bi?*

She thinks it's cool, I tell her. *Know what she said? You could have had anybody and chose me.*

Oh the Fear I've Known

The greatest challenge of this semester, I write in my Advanced Fiction Workshop journal, *may well be how to stay in love and write at the same time.*

An image of Professor Snow, my workshop leader, is in my head as I write. She's standing in the packed reading room at Writers House, bay windows behind her, introducing another writer to the crowd. Her daughter, who's maybe three, ambles up mid-way through and tugs on her skirt. Professor Snow leans down to pick her up. She brushes a curl off her daughter's face, gives her the attention she needs in a physical way, all the while remaining poised and attentive to the audience. She pauses speaking only for that moment when her voice would be projected into the floor. She makes it look like introductions are meant to be given with a small child in your arms reaching for your earring. In a way, this is the perfect image of the balance I'm striving for.

Thanks to Advanced Placement credits, I'm enrolled as a part-time student this semester, which is saving my parents a few thousand dollars of tuition and providing me subsidized time to write before I graduate. Time that, so far, I have instead been using to talk and write to my girlfriend, who is now back on email again.

MAP   65

I think back to the first occasion I made time like this to write, the summer between sophomore and junior years. I knew then, instinctively, that I had to choose between a potential relationship and my writing, and that I had to break things off with Jake if I truly wanted to find out how far I could take my writing with no obligations in the way. I defied my parents' expectations by not getting an internship, declared financial independence for the summer by using savings to sublet a room off-campus. It was a choosing of self, a recognition and acknowledgement, a commitment: my writing is the most important thing in my life.

That summer, mornings and evenings were driven by this passion of mine. Time and focus became a completed draft of a novel, a few stories, and a realistic sense of me as a writer. I joined two workshops for community and feedback. I can still remember the feeling as I walked around campus at the beginning of the next semester, hearing about other people's summer vacations and reflecting on my own, knowing I'd made the right decision. Knowing it was the best thing I'd ever done for myself.

Yet the lyrics of Emily Saliers' *Language or the Kiss* have been theming through my head ever since. ....*oh the fear I've known that I might reap the praise of strangers and end up on my own....* My writing is the single most important thing in my life, but alone it's not enough. That summer in all its rightness was also filled with lonely nights when the words wouldn't come, and days when they came fast and furious and there was no one there to hear them. There were dinners where I was the awkward third, and there was not knowing exactly where to go when my house was broken into. Lose my writing and I lose me, I know this. Lose me and any relationship is doomed, I know this too. Lose Catrina... I am not willing to let that happen for the sake of a single story. If I can learn in this semester how to strike a balance, how to write while being in love, then I'll be the closest I've ever been to a future with both. *If I fail,* I write in my journal, *I may lose the best story I ever could have written, but it's time to take that risk.*

As the end of class that afternoon, when Professor Snow asks who wants to hand out work next week, I volunteer. I ask Catrina not to call me the next day so I can concentrate on my writing, and in the morning, I grab the most recent draft of my story and my backpack and my hat and gloves and earmuffs and bike downtown.

The cold burns my throat, but the snow is all melted so it's a smooth ride. I'm not sure why I wind up at the Food Court in Liberty Place, why I felt the urge to bike today, but once I've eaten a slice of pizza and drunk most of my giant cup of water, I'm focused. I'm far from temptation, drawn in to the story on the pages in front of me, scribbling away.

I'm working on a story I started this past summer called "On the Eighth Day." My character Zack is marrying a non-Jewish woman, and this part of the story resonates more personally now. How will Zack and his wife raise their family? How will Catrina and I raise ours? I grew up thinking I'd have to marry someone Jewish because I'd need that shared background in a marriage, but lately I'm more interested in the meshing of differences.

Catrina says that feminism and poverty are basically her culture, the way Judaism is mine, in terms of how they have affected her life and how she defines herself. When she frames it that way, it doesn't bother me how little she knows about Judaism—instead, I realize how much I have to learn too. I'm

MAP 67

excited for us to teach each other, to figure out how to honor both our heritages with integrity and let faith be truly personal. Maybe I can use this story to share my ideas with Catrina.

I imagine Zack's interpretation of a Shabbat dinner, blending his wife's family tradition with the Jewish blessings of his childhood. I write for an hour, two hours, three. The pages are scribbled on all over, front and back. I need to type this into my computer to go any further. It feels good though. A little typing, maybe a few more small changes, and this story will be ready for workshopping. I bike home to type the changes, then print out the new draft and read it over, not letting myself check email before I'm sure the draft is ready. I feel good. I've done it. Writing, quality writing, while I'm in a relationship. *Enhanced*, even, by the experience of the relationship. It was only one afternoon, but for now, it's enough.

Looking back years later as a more seasoned writer, one privileged to witness the ongoing artistic journeys of others along with my own, I will know that this balancing act of writing and relationships is something that most of us as writers will engage with throughout our lives. I will be intrigued that, despite how much I thought I wanted to be with someone, somehow I knew when Jake came along that I wasn't ready yet. I will appreciate the sturdy foundation I built by early immersion in art and self, as well as the understanding that it is engagement with others which adds the richness and texture to what comes next.

How Far?

I haven't broken my promise to Tyler not to tell anyone about her and Heather, but my perceptive girlfriend has figured out that something is up.

Please tell me, Catrina begs.

I can't, I say, not for the first time. *I promised.*

Please?

Hey, why don't we call Tyler? I propose. I'm hoping that Tyler will tell Catrina herself, and that's exactly what happens, with no prompting from me.

Mostly I just listen while the two of them talk. It's nice to be quiet and hear Tyler and Catrina getting along. It's like they've talked a million times before, rather than just emailed a couple of times to trade bootlegs.

Oh, I have a girlfriend too, Catrina says, when she's run out of other answers to *what's new.*

Really? says Tyler, playing along. *What's she like?*

Well, she goes to Penn, she's a writer, we met online. She keeps promising to visit but she hasn't gotten tickets yet, so I don't know.

I laugh. But it occurs to me that Tyler might be the first person Catrina has told about *our* relationship.

A couple of hours later Catrina is telling us how you can go

MAP   69

into any hairdresser in Olympia and ask for Dyke Haircut #3—which I picture in my head as the one I wanted last fall, short but long enough to run your fingers through—when Tyler's call waiting beeps for the fourth or fifth time, and Tyler says she really ought to get off the phone.

Tyler says goodnight and hangs up, and Catrina stays on the phone. It only takes a moment for it to be intense again, the two of us just listening to each other breathe, being together that way.

Time disappears for a while into Catrina's inhale-exhale. My own breath flows in rhythm with hers, a rhythm that is becoming increasingly arousing, slower and deeper. Then I shift my position because my leg is starting to cramp up and there's a loud thump.

What was that? Catrina asks.

I don't know. I lean over the edge of the bed and look. *Oh, my backpack. No big deal.*

The mood is already disrupted, so I reach to pick up the papers which have fallen out. In the lull, a question returns, and I decide to ask it. *Is Tyler the first person you told about me?*

Kind of, Catrina says. *Well, except for Heidi from the Indigo Girls list. And I told my roommate we had mutual crushes on each other, because she was asking why I'm on the phone so much, but she's still a little weird about me being gay, so I didn't say anything else.*

I'm not sure how to feel. Doesn't Catrina want to run and skip and jump all over Olympia, singing out her love for me so all can hear? Am I allowed to wish she'd tell more people? Would *I* be as open as I am if I were in her shoes? Should I just feel grateful for my own email-savvy, gay-friendly pals?

Tyler's really nice, Catrina says sleepily.

Yeah, I say, yawning. I want to say more to Catrina about Tyler, about how our friendship is starting to grow, but I realize I'm too exhausted all of a sudden to get the words out.

The next Friday night Tyler comes over for dinner. Since Tyler's Jewish, I defrost the *challah* my dad sent back with me and use the extra wine from the chicken florentine to say *kiddush.* Shabbat for me is a state of mind, a ritual that happens when I am home with my family or gathered with other Jews. When I'm racing off to a concert, or alone for dinner, it's just a Friday. It's nice to make tonight into Shabbat.

As we eat, I tell Tyler more about the night Catrina and I fell in love, and Tyler tells me how she and Heather got together. Until now I've only heard bits and pieces of the story, but even so I'm the only person at Penn who knows that Tyler and Heather are dating.

One day on email, Tyler says, *I wrote how I'd always wanted to kiss a girl, and Heather wrote back* I would kiss you. *That's how it started.*

I don't say anything, but I'm looking at Tyler so she knows I'm listening.

We walked all the way to the football stadium on her next visit, Tyler says, *and went behind a huge support beam, and I made sure that no one was around. I was so scared of anyone finding out. Heather asked what I thought of the location and then asked me if I was sure I wanted to do this a couple of times, and then we kissed.*

I tell Tyler about Jake. Tyler tells me about the prom at her high school, and then about a guy she kind of went out with last fall. I tell her about the Tom Cruise look-alike camp counselor I had a crush on for two years. I think about how being in a relationship strengthens your friendships too, because of the urge to share stories.

MAP   71

The first guy I ever hooked up with was twenty-eight, I say.

How old were you? Tyler asks.

Nineteen. He was my tutor. With practice you can make any-thing sound nonchalant. Separate the telling from the emotions. *I didn't do anything unsafe, but I was this close.*

I hold up my thumb and forefinger about an inch apart. *This close. I used to watch all those videos in middle school and high school about kids getting pregnant and getting AIDS and think, how stupid can you be? but I didn't realize how quickly you can go there from just standing and talking.*

I am telling this to Tyler as though it is a war story, a close call where one comes out unscathed, but that is far from the truth, though I'm still not able to comprehend quite how far.

It had started as a frustrating-yet-comfortable crush on some-one unattainable, one like many I'd had on teachers and camp counselors since age fourteen. He was the tutor recommended and introduced to me by the university, for a subject I needed to pass in order to graduate. All I'd hoped for was some sign that the feelings didn't only go one way. Then he was in my bed. It happened at the end of a tutoring session. Him naked without asking, me voiceless, him leaving parts of my body raw and scabbed. Someone told me later, *he has herpes, he gave it to me.* Panicked, I examined the edges of my mouth over and over in the mirror for the telltale cold sores. I asked questions at the university health center that no one seemed to be able to answer. I wondered how much worse it might have been if I hadn't found the words to say in the midst *I haven't done this before* and we had done *that.*

Next year, I'll write about the incident in a fiction workshop and the workshop leader will refer to what happened as a near-rape experience and I will feel validated. It will take much longer to begin to understand that many people aren't like the tutor and instead truly do want to communicate and take it slow. Longer still to understand how this trauma added to the internet's appeal to me, even while I wasn't looking for the love I found there. I'll stumble across a definition in a book called *Where to Draw the Line* by someone named Anne Katherine: *Boundaries give you safety without making you miss out on the good stuff.* Of course. Naturally I would feel more comfortable, find it easier to open up and get to know someone, in a medium where distance and intimacy combined in a physically safe way. Naturally I would find it easier to grow in a place that provided boundaries I had not yet learned to create on my own.

Did you like women back then? Tyler asks, as I put my last forkful of dinner in my mouth. *Because when I look back I keep recognizing these crushes I had, not that I thought they were crushes at the time, I just thought they were cool people, but now I see them as crushes.*

I finish chewing and swallowing before I answer. She's watching me, expectant, and I want to come through for her but I don't want to lie. *I don't think so,* I say. I can't tell if she's disappointed. *All these friends—guy friends, mostly—were coming out a couple of years ago, and I started thinking about it because of that. And then I saw a couple of movies, and books, and it was just around. I don't know. I really wanted to have some experience with guys, physical hooking up experience. The strange thing is that a friend I met freshman year said last week he's known I was bi for three years.*

Weird, says Tyler. *How did he know?*

He said it was gaydar, which he apparently has even though he's straight. I just don't get it. I mean, I don't look like the stereotype, and I understand you can tell sometimes if someone's gay and

MAP 73

repressing it, but I don't think I was repressing anything. I shrug. *He said I should ask Matthew to explain it to me.*

After we finish eating, we move into my bedroom, where Tyler flips through my CDs and then my photo album from Israel. It feels good to be hanging out in person. It's restful–fingertips not clenched up at a keyboard, shoulder not cramped holding a phone, interaction not so completely dependent on language. It's also an affirmation that our friendship bridges the two worlds I've been inhabiting all year, the old Penn world of brick and bodies and this new world of electronic mailing lists and lesbians and love.

I pull out my high school yearbook to show Tyler what I looked like four years ago. Near the beginning, there's a picture I took of this woman who was the epitome of cool. Smart, class president, athlete, musician. She was popular in the effortless-seeming way that most eludes me and yet still someone worth engaging with in English class. Studying her picture, I recall the rumors I've heard about how she shaved her head and came out her freshman year of college. She wasn't someone I hung out with, and I'd never really understood why I was so interested in finding out whether the rumor was true. I wonder if maybe I'm wrong in what I told Tyler a little while ago. *Her,* I say to Tyler, pointing. *Maybe I did have a crush or two back then.*

As I'm pointing out my senior page to Tyler, the phone rings. It's Matthew. I put him on speaker phone.

Explain gaydar to me, I demand. *How did Kevin know three years ago that I was bi?*

It's gaydar, Matthew says. *It just is.*

Could you tell about me? I ask.

No, he says, *I was too busy hiding myself in the closet. My own gaydar is a more recent development. Jake picked up on it, though. He was the one who suggested fixing you up with Marcie Roberts.*

Jake—what? I don't have any more words.

How did Jake figure it out? Tyler asks. *Audrey doesn't look gay.*

Yeah, but she listens to too much folk music to be straight.

I was raised on folk music, I say. *You can't tell from that.* Then I ask, *Did Jake think I was actually gay?*

He knew you were bi, Matthew assures me, but that doesn't make me feel any better. How did Jake figure it out in the first place? Can a guy tell something like that from hooking up with you?

The one guy I ever kissed couldn't tell, Catrina says, later that evening.

You kissed a guy?

Yeah, once. My friend Patrick. I got bored with it after ten minutes, that's how I knew I was a lesbian.

Oh. How come he got to kiss you and I haven't? I make my voice sound super-jealous.

If you get on the next plane, we can change that. You can kiss me good morning.

Okay, I agree, not moving from my bed. Outside I can hear the wind tunnel blowing through the high rises, but it's hot inside the dorm so I have a window cracked open and I'm lying on top of my comforter. *How many girls have you kissed?*

Two.

She describes them both and now I really *am* jealous, partly because they've kissed her, partly because she's kissed girls and I haven't. I don't say anything though.

What are you thinking about? she asks.

You. What you'll look like naked.

MAP   75

Somehow I know she's smiling on the other end.

I love you, I say.

I love you too, she says. Then she says, *I'm cute naked.*

I believe you.

I bet you're cute naked too.

Now I'm the one smiling. I think maybe why I love her so much is that she brings out these parts of me. The cute parts. The beautiful parts. Somehow her faith that they exist makes them appear in a way they never have before.

And it doesn't really matter that she's kissed girls and I haven't, or that I liked kissing boys and she didn't. Because right now both of us want to kiss each other, and more.

What My Girlfriend Looks Like Naked

It finally dawns on me that I can rearrange my work schedule and get five days off in a row on any given week. Not quite as much as spring break, but close. I want to know what my girlfriend looks like naked. Know that like no one else ever has.

The next time we talk, I ask Catrina to pull out a calendar and look at dates, and the day after that, I visit a travel agent. I get plane tickets for the sixth to the tenth of February. I'm really going.

Only fourteen days! Catrina emails me that night. *I think that if I were to wake up to you every morning for the rest of my life I would be in a continual state of bliss and happiness.*

She forwards me a copy of an email she sent to a friend of hers, which starts off, *so, the girl. Her name is Audrey. Remember that story I forwarded to you? She wrote that. She's absolutely brilliant. If I weren't so damn wonderful myself, I would think she is too good for me.*

I'm blushing as I read, and calmed as it sinks in that Catrina's telling people about me now. *Deep in my heart,* Catrina says towards the end of the email, *I just think she is the one. I've never felt anything this intense in my life. And I suppose it is all quite crazy because we have never met. But I've seen pictures. And if we are not immediately attracted to each other, we think it will grow.*

MAP 77

On the phone that night, Catrina mentions that Dar Williams is playing in Seattle that weekend. *Want to go?* she asks. *Our first date?*

I'd love to, I say.

I ask how cold it will be in Seattle, which jacket I should pack. We start planning which day to drive down to Oregon to see Sasha. We decide I'll order the concert tickets since Catrina's credit card is maxed out, and she'll pick them up and then pay me back for hers before my Visa bill comes. Catrina tells me that her roommate has volunteered to make herself scarce during my visit, so we can have plenty of time to ourselves.

I'm eating cookie dough ice cream as we talk. Catrina's eating peanut butter out of the jar. *For protein,* she says. *It was another iceberg lettuce day at work.* She tells me she can't go grocery shopping until her next paycheck and that the food supply in her apartment is almost depleted. I can't quite fathom this. My parents give me an allowance for food and there's always money in the bank. Even if it's money I'm not supposed to spend, it's there.

I'm not really sure what to do. I feel helpless, all these miles away.

Catrina is telling me not to worry, this has happened before, payday is only in three days. How can I not worry? If she were here, I'd invite her over for dinner, make sure she ate a decent meal. *Let me buy you groceries,* I suggest.

No. She won't let me, not even as a loan. I offer again over email. She refuses again, stubborn, says she won't let anyone help. *Especially when that person is my girlfriend,* she says, *and the woman I want to spend the rest of my life with. I don't want something as stupid as money to screw that up.*

I'm not strong enough to make her change her mind. I can

barely eat for the next three days because all I can think about is her starving, subsisting on nothing but Ramen noodles and peanut butter.

To: Tyler
Subject: coming out to parents
Date: Thu, 23 Jan 1997 12:54:22 -0500 (EST)

[what would i say?] uhhh, mom, i have never met this person in my life, but i fell in love on email and we're even thinking about getting married, oh, and she's a girl......

nope. don't think that's the best way to do it. once i am there, i can say that we are kinda interested in each other, and we became friends through email, and since i am going to be in seattle anyway then maybe something might come of it. much easier for my parents to digest that way, i think.

I tell my parents that I am going there to decide if I want to live in Seattle after I graduate, and to visit Sasha, and to visit Catrina, who invited me to crash at her apartment.

Catrina calls me to report that she got paid and bought groceries. *You can stop worrying,* she says. She narrates each grocery item as she puts it into her fridge.

On Tuesday, a week before I'm set to fly, I call my mom's best friend Rhonda. I want Mom to have someone to talk to after I call her from Seattle. *Can I ask you a question?*

Sure, she answers.

Does my mom know I'm bisexual?

Well, Rhonda says. *What a question.*

We laugh together for a few seconds.

MAP   79

Your mother is a perceptive woman, Rhonda says.

Rhonda and I chat for a while. She tells me about her specula-tions about her own daughter's sexual orientation. She tells me about how her son flew to visit an old flame once and how she was worried but understood he had to do it. I've never talked to a parent about what they think about their kids before, and it's neat. *If you called me about this,* Rhonda says, *you must want your mom to know. Go ahead, tell her.*

I hang up and blast the Indigo Girls on my stereo to clear my head. I want to get the impending conversation with Mom out of my mind, so I'll just blurt out something naturally. If I just blurt out something small, like the fact that I have a date with Catrina to go a Dar Williams concert, then Mom can just be like *that's nice, who's Dar Williams?* instead of immediately asking all the other questions I don't have answers to yet.

I wish I had already told my parents, back at the beginning of winter vacation when all I would have had to say was, *I might date a woman sometime.*

On Wednesday evening I join a bunch of friends for dinner in the dining hall. Before I bought the plane ticket, these friends seemed supportive of my relationship, asking to see the pic-tures, telling me their favorite internet romance stories. Today they take turns warning me. *You can't be sure what you're getting into. What if you decide the first night that you can't stand each other in person? Do you know anyone else out there? You should bring extra cash.*

I'm not stupid, I want to say. *I already know all the damn risks.* I know how to dial 9-1-1 or call a cab or rent a hotel if things get weird. I'll have a credit card and a MAC card and plenty of money in my checking account. My best friend will be two hours away. There are other people from the Indigo Girls list in the area. Catrina has already filled me in on her sexual history—nonexistent, other than kissing, so she's safe—and we've decided to take that whole thing as it comes. *I have a good sense of judgment,* I say instead. *I can take care of myself.*

I feel this huge need to touch Catrina, to feel her hand in mine and to finally kiss. In my mind, touch is like the autograph of a famous person you met in a blur, or a ticket stub, or a stone from the top of a mountain you climbed. If something happened and Catrina and I had never had any sort of physical contact, it would be too easy for it to feel like a good book of fiction when I looked back. When you're inside a piece of good fiction it's real, but when you emerge, you know it was only a story. Knowing the feel of Catrina's skin will make this somehow more real.

I'm getting anxious. I'm getting scared, not of meeting her, but of what could possibly happen in the next eight days to thwart the meeting. I think about Catrina running out of food again. I think about car accidents, unexpected family emergencies, snowstorms. I imagine a funeral, being afraid to look inside the casket and see Catrina for the first time dead, afraid to kiss her, afraid not to, afraid to tell her family who I am.

I have a dream Wednesday night that when we meet, both of our families are there. Her dad is driving the car, and our moms are chatting away. We're sitting in the back under the watchful eyes of her sisters, and I'm not even able to touch her hand. I keep looking at her whenever she's staring out the window or talking to her sisters, thinking about how close we are and imagining touching her face. *Wait until we get back to Olympia and we're alone,* she says, but I wake up before we get there.

Telling

Are you telling me you're a lesbian? Mom asks. Her words are clear and distinct, as though she's in the front of a classroom.

There's no way to hide in the back row, give a half-answer, let her redirect the question to someone else. *I'm telling you I'm bisexual.*

It's not what I want to say. It's not true. I *am* bisexual but I was *telling* her about me being interested in Catrina, which *is* true although it's probably the understatement of the year. But Mom says, *Thank you for telling me. I love you.* And what else can I say then but *I love you too.*

It's Thursday and it was four o'clock in the afternoon when I got interrupted by the phone ringing. I sensed as soon as I heard Mom's voice and saw the time and found out my dad wasn't home that this was going to be the conversation when it happened.

Mom had a lame excuse for her call, asking what hotel they should stay at for graduation, a question that easily could have waited until the rates changed and Dad got home. After we had the usual introductory how-are-you conversation, she asked me to tell her more about Catrina. Since Catrina was obviously important to me, and I was going out to visit her, and, well, we began corresponding over email.

I tried. But it was hard. The facts are weird, and I couldn't just be like *well, she's graduated, looking for waitressing jobs* and leave it at that, because it doesn't sound like Catrina has her shit together when I explain it that way.

So finally there was this long pause. I knew there was no turning back without putting myself in this closet I say I'm not in.

Well, I'm kind of interested in her, I said.

We figured something was going on when we saw the phone bill, Mom tells me now. *We're not stupid.* She asks more about my travel plans, backup plans, contact information in case of emergency.

I tell her I'll email all the contact information and flight schedules before I leave. I tell her I'll look up hotel and youth hostel information before I go, just in case. I remind her that I know how to call 9-1-1. I tell her not to worry.

I'm a mother, she says. *It's my job to worry. I'd be worried if you were flying across the country and staying with a boy you had an emotional involvement with.*

You'd be more worried that way, probably, I say.

I just don't want to see my daughter get hurt, she says.

I think the hard part is over, and I'm relieved. Typing lightly so Mom can't hear, I send a quick email to Catrina and Tyler, *My mom's on the phone—I just came out to her. More later.*

Mom's next questions all hint at *do you have any experience.* It's hard to figure out how to be honest without telling more than I'm comfortable telling.

I want to know about you, she says. *You're my daughter. I want to understand.*

Um, I say. *What exactly do you want to know?*

MAP   83

Well, she asks, *are you dating women? Have you dated women?*

I say defensively, *the only dates I've been on that you would call dates were with Jake.*

What happened with Jake? she asks. *Is this why you called it off? Did he know you were bisexual?*

No, I tell her. *I ended it because I was writing a novel that summer, you knew that.*

I thought there might have been another reason you hadn't mentioned.

Nope.

Mom asks about other guys she knows about, all the way back to Paul from summer camp in sixth grade. There's already an email in my box from Tyler, *Congratulations! How did it go? Call and tell me when you get off the phone.* I try to answer Mom's questions without letting on that those are the only guys I've been involved with. The only person she misses is Jay, who I kissed in fourth grade. Thankfully she doesn't bring up the tutor. Then she asks, *Is Catrina—experienced?*

I'm not exactly comfortable discussing Catrina's sexual history with my mom. *I don't think it's my place to answer that,* I say instead.

Mom seems a little taken aback. Score one for Audrey. She pauses, then asks if I'm sure about all this—*all this* meaning *being bisexual*—or still wondering. She says it sounds like I'm still wondering, or questioning. I tell her I'm not, I'm sure. I don't know if she believes that or not. *Are you happy?* she asks.

Yes, I say. What am I supposed to say, that I'd rather not be having this conversation? That I'm uncomfortable with her questions? In self-defense I try to flip the tables on her. *Are you happy?* I ask.

She's kind of obviously thrown by the question, like she

doesn't understand how her happiness relates to this subject. *I'm happy if you're happy,* she says carefully.

My dad gets home at this point and picks up the phone. Mom and I pause the conversation long enough to say hi, and then Mom somehow convinces Dad to get off the phone and go in another room until we're done talking, *no, nothing's wrong, we were just in the middle of a mother-daughter conversation.*

Dad says he'll talk to me later and hangs up, and then the conversation gets more awkward. Mom wants to know how long I've known. I'm still not sure of the answer to that question. What answer is she looking for? Is it better in her eyes if I've known forever and not told her, or just figured it out? She makes it sound like there's a rule about how much time is supposed to elapse between figuring it out and telling her. She makes it sound like I'm already convicted of breaking the rule. I want to change the subject. Why does it matter how long I've known?

My intellectual belief that I'm searching for a soulmate rather than a gender is something I'm sure I would have agreed with at age seventeen or even age five if anyone asked. The deck of cards with naked women which I used to look at with a flashlight in my closet as a kid is probably best attributed to basic pre-adolescent curiosity, just like the Chippendales cards with bare-chested male dancers I bought at the mall a few years later. Attraction? Desire? I don't know if they just showed up one day, if they were triggered by movies, if they've been hiding out forever and then slowly appeared. I'm in love, that's what matters.

I don't really know, Mom, I say. I fumble through a few more sentences, not saying anything new but trying to keep her from responding with *what do you mean, you don't really know.* I wish I

MAP   85

could try to flip the tables again, but it feels too intrusive to ask these kinds of questions about Mom and Dad. Maybe I'm scared to find out some of the answers.

Mom wants to know who else knows, am I *out?* I sense more behind that question: *Am I the last to know? Why? Don't you care about me? Don't you trust me? Let me in.*

Out is relative, I tell her. I know she'll be hurt if she finds out how many random people know, and I can't lie, so I stick to vagueness. She asks if Sasha knows, and if Matthew knows. I tell her she should talk to her friend Rhonda, that I talked to Rhonda the other night. She's touched by that.

Is it okay if I tell people? she asks. *I'm not planning to advertise, but if it comes up in conversation...*

It's fine with me, I tell her, *as soon as Dad is comfortable with it.*

It turns out Mom has already told Dad on a few occasions that she suspected I was a lesbian. Dad has brushed off the idea. He thinks Mom is making it up. This surprises me—both Mom's bringing up the topic and Dad's reaction.

Mom thinks I need to tell Dad.

I was planning to wait until I got to Seattle to tell you both, I say.

I think he'll be hurt if you wait that long, Mom says. *Can I put him on the phone?*

No, I say. *You can tell him,* I say.

He won't believe me. She says he needs to hear the words *Dad, I am bisexual,* coming from my mouth. And he needs to hear them soon.

This isn't what I expected. Coming out to my dad isn't something my *mom* should be choreographing.

What's he going to say? I ask, suddenly nervous.

Audrey, you're the pride and joy of his life. Mom pauses. *It's not like you're telling him you just won a scholarship, but I think you're worrying unnecessarily.*

Mom?

Yes?

Remember last year when I told you about hooking up with the tutor, and how that was what was making me so stressed about going abroad and passing my language proficiency exam?

Mmhm.

And I wanted Dad to know so he'd get off my case about my application, but I didn't know how to tell him about it, and you said not to worry, you promised to handle Dad on that sort of thing?

Audrey, that was a very different situation. You need to do this yourself.

I can't believe she's going back on her word. That just doesn't happen in our family. I was counting on her. *Mom, you promised. If you want him to know now, you can tell him.*

We go back and forth. We finally agree that she will tell him first, and that I will call in the next forty-eight hours to tell him myself. Before we hang up she asks again if she can put him on the phone. I say *no.* I'm not ready. I need the guts.

I call Catrina.

It's me. Did you get my email?

No, I haven't checked it since this morning.

I just came out to my mom.

You did? Catrina sounds surprised. *I thought you weren't planning to tell them yet.*

I tell Catrina how the conversation transpired.

Her reactions seem *off* somehow, although I can't quite put

MAP   87

my finger on it. Is Catrina feeling pressure to tell *her* parents? I don't ask.

Today was my last day of work, she says, which I'd forgotten. *No more serving dead animals to obnoxious yuppies.* Maybe that's it. Catrina changed around her plans a few days ago, deciding not to take the job she'd lined up at the new vegetarian cafe after all. *I still don't know what I'm doing next, she says.*

There's always temping, I say. *It probably pays more than waitressing.*

I'm not working in an office, she says.

A bookstore? I suggest. *It's always been one of my fantasies. You could learn more about the book business before you start your own.*

Doesn't pay enough. Besides, they're not hiring.

I keep trying to offer helpful suggestions, even offer to help her redo her resume, but my suggestions don't seem to be helping. *You'll figure it out,* I say.

Maybe. Catrina doesn't sound convinced. She sounds more like she wants to crawl into a cave and hibernate.

After we hang up, I pull my phone into the living room and nosh on cheese and crackers as I tell Tyler all about the conversation with Mom. She asks a lot of questions, like she's taking notes for when it's her turn.

I email Catrina that evening, *do you want me to give you space this weekend? Not call or email?*

Yes, thank you, Catrina writes back. *You are so nice. We can talk again on Sunday night. I don't want to not talk to you but I think I need some space right now. Everything is so jumbled and confusing right now in my life, unemployment and where am I going to live and everything, and the thought of forever freaks me out. I know I'm not saying this well. I love you and I'm sure I will be back to normal and missing you greatly by Sunday afternoon. If you miss me a lot, go listen to the song Sure Thing on the mix I gave you, that's how I feel. And if it's an emergency, you can call. Like if you come out to your dad.*

In the morning I look at the date on my computer and realize my parents' anniversary is tomorrow. I need to come out to Dad *today.* Damn. Anniversaries are for *happy anniversary, I love you, thanks for getting married and being my parents. Not for I'm bi or I'm interested in this woman I met online.* Deep breath.

Goodbye, Daddy's little girl.

I'll need to figure out what to say. I'll need to wait a few hours for Dad to get home from work. I'll need someone to talk to afterwards.

Tyler has rush events all afternoon. Matthew has an academic crisis to deal with and then a date tonight. Catrina needs space.

I start chasing down my remaining friends—AJ, the few dorm-mates who aren't going to see *Star Wars* tonight, people from Writers House, Derek out in Colorado. *If I come out to my dad at three o'clock, can you be around for the post-coming-out vent-ing cooldown? How about four-thirty?* Eventually I get the whole afternoon and evening covered.

Good luck, Derek says, after telling me when he'll be near his phone. *I really wish I wasn't so far away, or I'd drive over there to be with you.*

Yesterday, before Mom called, I had been reading Penn's weekly entertainment magazine, *34th Street,* when I came to a review of a new TV show I've never seen called *Relativity.* The reviewer devoted the whole piece to one episode where two

MAP   89

women kiss, turning the review into a top ten list where eight of the ten reasons why the show is good were some obnoxious variation of *two girls kissing...need I say more?* I wasn't surprised to see a male name in the byline. I decided I needed to write a response, and that response is what I had just started writing when Mom called. Now I decide that I need to finish the piece before I call Dad. Since I often read my writing to my father, I'm hoping this piece can be a natural segue to the conversation.

I pack up my Powerbook and go to Writers House, petting Lucid on my way in. An acquaintance and a stranger are sitting on my favorite couch in the living room, talking. People are walking in and out. The acquaintance sees me and asks, *what's up,* and then, *what's wrong.*

The story starts spilling out.

You might want to talk a little quieter, the acquaintance suggests mid-way through my telling, and I realize there's a class or meeting or something in the adjacent dining room. I've probably just come out to a dozen more people.

I feel exposed. I keep talking loudly, a kind of offense-as-defense protection. At camp in tenth grade when I found out people had read my diary, I started reading parts aloud, handing it to people. Somehow I felt less violated that way, although it didn't take away the fact of exposure.

After I finish the story, I ask the stranger, *what's your name?* We laugh, and she introduces herself. And then the acquaintance looks at her watch and apologizes and says that the two of them need to leave for class. I'm thankful they waited until I finished talking.

I plug in my Powerbook in another corner and open the file called *Relativity review response.*

I run my fingers along the curves of the keyboard, letting the raised bumps on the *D* and *K* keys tickle my middle fingers. I've decided to use the offensive article as a catalyst to talk about larger issues, rather than give it more attention than it deserves. *What disturbs me,* I write, *is that the editorial staff thought this article appropriate for this publication and that many otherwise intelligent students found it funny. One of the great things about popular media is that they offer a way to change American consciousness...If you don't know anyone gay personally, your idea of what a gay person is like is probably largely shaped by your knowledge of people who are out in a very loud, in-your-face kind of way. Quality television can help provide a balance. A lesbian character on a sitcom is visibly out not only when she is participating in a gay pride march but also when she is ordering food in a restaurant.*

It's quiet and I'm maybe two-thirds of the way through when the woman who runs Writers House comes over and says there's going to be a reading soon in the other room, *could you move upstairs please?*

I'm sorry, I can't, I say as politely as I can. *I wish I could, but I can't, I have to finish this. I'll be quiet, I'll be out of here as soon as I'm done.*

I would really appreciate it if you would move, she says in a bitchy voice.

Can't she see that I am panicked, that these aren't normal circumstances? I look back to my screen. I have maybe a couple of paragraphs left but if I lose my focus, it won't get done.

They can hear the typing, she says next, which I know is bullshit. I ignore her and try to concentrate on the words in front of me, and eventually she goes away. I finish only a couple of minutes after the reading starts. I sit for another twenty minutes. Partly for spite. Mostly to compose myself, read over the essay, make a few minor changes, and regain my courage.

MAP   91

I pack up quietly, not looking at anyone, and leave Writers House. I realize I'm hungry, so I stop at Chats. AJ's there. She gives me a free raspberry coffee drink along with my burrito, and I give her the Cliff's Notes on the last couple of days. AJ has to rush off to an *a cappella* rehearsal after her shift ends, but she wishes me luck telling my dad and invites me to go to the movies with a bunch of people tomorrow night.

My mom has followed through on her promise, so at 8:22, when I finally go back to my room and make the call, my father already knows I'm bisexual.

I read Dad what I've been writing and then ask, *can you tell I'm bisexual from the article?* I don't wait for an answer before continuing, *because it shouldn't matter. To the reader, I mean. So long as you know I'm bisexual, that's important.*

You think you are, he says first. I let that pass. *Mommy told me. Thanks for telling me.* He's sincere and I try to decide if it's appropriate to say *you're welcome* but he keeps talking. *As you can probably guess, I'm not exactly thrilled, but I wouldn't be thrilled if you broke your leg either...you're still my favorite daughter and I still love you.*

I burst out laughing at the strangeness of his broken leg analogy. *You're funny,* I say. *I love you too.*

Dad doesn't have any questions for me like Mom did, so we start talking about computers. For the next twenty minutes he tells me about the latest developments on the computer program he's been writing to keep track of our family tree, the one which doesn't automatically give a space for *husband* anymore when you say *female.*

What about the article? I ask, when we finish with all the tangent conversation. *You never answered my question, can you tell that I'm bi from the article?*

I don't think so, he says. *But I'd still advise you against publishing it. You don't want to go looking for attention.*

What about everything you taught me about activism and standing up for yourself? You write letters to the editor all the time.

Uh uh, he says, meaning this isn't a valid parallel. His tone signals that he's on the verge of stubborn mode. Stubborn mode is what happens when he doesn't have a response, and when Dad gets into stubborn mode, there's no arguing with him—he doesn't know how to concede. *Once something is published, you can't take it back.*

Like I said, Dad, what about everything you publish?

That's different, he says. *There are a lot of crazy people out there.*

My father is definitely in stubborn mode. He writes letters to the editor for the newspaper of our Republican, conservative, very Roman Catholic city, supporting Israel and condemning the placement of a nativity scene on city property. That's far more controversial than a pro-gay article on a Democratic, liberal, forty percent Jewish college campus.

I try to reason with Dad, but it's not working and when he says that even publishing the piece anonymously is asking for trouble, I decide to just let him talk, knowing I'm my father's daughter and I'm not going to back down because of what he says in stubborn mode.

Think hard about if you really want to do this, Dad says at the end of the conversation. *There are other ways to take action without putting yourself at risk.*

Dad's last point sounds more like rational counsel than an over-protective father's feeble control tactics, and so I agree to consider it.

MAP   93

My mom gets on at the end of the phone call to say *hi* and remind me to email them my itinerary and call before I leave for Seattle. When I get off the phone, I'm breathing calmly for the first time since Thursday afternoon.

If I'm Falling Down

The calm doesn't last. An email arrives with the subject line *lots of shit*. It's from Tyler. *My roommate came home unexpectedly this morning when Heather and I were sleeping*, it begins, and gets worse from there. *She just grabbed a book and left, and when I got back just now she was asleep, but I know she knows about us. Then, at lunch, one of the people I'm planning to live with next year said that it would make her uncomfortable if her roommate was gay. Oh, and my best friend said her roommate's boyfriend always sleeps in their room and that makes her uncomfortable. I can imagine how she'd feel if it was a girl. But I really want to tell her about me.*

Definitely *lots of shit*. I want to go over to Tyler's dorm right now and somehow make it all better. I want to give her my friends who asked to see pictures of my girlfriend, my mom who said *I love you*. Because of the sleeping roommate factor, I can't even reach out to her by phone. I start writing Tyler back, hoping that something I say will help, because words are all I have to offer.

Derek calls while I'm typing away. *Did you tell your dad?*

Once I actually dialed the phone, it was pretty easy.

Thank God. You had me worried this morning.

I type *Derek just called, more in a few,* and send Tyler the

MAP   95

unfinished message in case her roommate wakes up in the next few minutes. I don't log out of my email account. I'm lying face-down on my bed with my computer resting on a chair by my head, the position I've been using to email Catrina and everyone else for the last few weeks.

As I tell Derek the story, I can see more email come in. There's one from Catrina, without a subject line. I wasn't expecting to hear from her until Sunday, and I'm tempted to look but I don't.

Derek and I keep talking for a while and then while he's speaking I hit the enter key like it's instinct and I see the first line, *Hi. Well. So I've been freaking out.*

Derek? I interrupt what he's saying. *Um, I've had my email on this whole time, and this thing just came in, and, oh shit.* I'm already panicking. I can't deal with the click of the phone right now, experiencing this alone and trying to explain what happened to other people after the fact. And so I hear as I read aloud to Derek the words my girlfriend is using to break up with me.

Hi. Well. So I've been freaking out. And I've come to the realiza-tion that I just can't do this relationship thing anymore. I can't deal with a relationship at this point in my life. It's too much. She says she just can't commit, doesn't want to hurt me but doesn't see a way around it, thinks I'm wonderful and amazing. She says she'll understand if I want to send her hate mail and never speak to her again. I'm numb by the last line. *I do love you, but I can only love you as a friend.*

Shit, Aud, Derek says, shock in his voice. *That's awful. Damn.*

She's breaking up with me. Catrina's breaking up with me. No. *No.* She can't do that. What about Seattle? Seeing her. Kissing her. Moving there. Us? Her emails, the *love me* without a comma. Her voice in my ear through the phone as I'm falling asleep. Her down pillows we're supposed to lay our heads on together this Thursday. Everything. All of it. Gone.

Derek stays on the phone. There's not much for either of us to say, but just knowing he's on the other end is comforting.

She's gone.

After a while Derek's fiancee gets home, and he has to let me go so he can make dinner. He does it gently, saying *Aud, you gonna be okay? I'll call you later—shit, I really wish I could be there.* He says this a couple of times like he really means it, he wishes he could be there. I try not to feel abandoned. I assure Derek that I'm not going to do anything drastic so it's safe for him to get off the phone, not sure if I'm saying it for his sake or mine. When I hear the dial tone, I set the receiver back in its cradle, stare at my computer screen, and try to think logically.

No tears yet. Just shock.

Can I wake up and make the email disappear?

Logically. Think logically.

I think about how Derek and his fiancee broke up once, before they got engaged. Maybe Catrina and I still have a chance. I try to imagine us back together this summer after she's sorted out the job and student loan situations. Then I think about Jake and how I'd told him two summers ago *talk to me in September.* By September he'd already found someone else. I need to focus on the short term.

I still have a plane ticket to Seattle. Catrina said I could still come. I'll do that. I'll fly out and we'll have everything once, only it'll be the end rather than the beginning. I remember this old question, from high school when all my friends were still virgins: *If you met your soulmate would you have sex on the first date?*

MAP   97

I would invariably answer *no, why rush things?* Savor it. But for the follow-up question *what if you'd never see the person again, this was the only time you'd ever have?* my answer was always *yes.* Savor that night.

I still have to finish that email to Tyler, do I tell her? I'm detached from the situation, it's me and the keys deciding the next move. Deciding whether to write Catrina back or call. When to do it. What to say. It's me and the keys deciding to postpone the decision, writing to Tyler instead like this didn't just happen. I type *sorry about the delay, more shit happening in my life but I will tell you another time,* and keep going. I take some pride in my composure, in my ability to think rationally.

I go back and read the email from yesterday afternoon that was Catrina's response to my question, *do you need space?* She'd said *listen to the song Sure Thing on the mix I gave you, that's how I feel.* I hadn't listened to it then. I'd been too stressed about telling Dad and I'd thought I'd have all weekend before hearing from Catrina again. Now I get the mix and read the liner and keep reading and reading and I can't find the song.

The next hours are a blur of more numbness, Catrina's mix in the background, reading emails, searching for clues of what to do next, more panic. I have to hear that song, I have to hear that song before I write back. Or call—dare I call? I don't know. The song, it's the missing part of this conversation, I can't continue until I find it. I pick up the cassette tape, eyes in and out of focus on Catrina's blue handwriting, willing the song to appear. It doesn't. I run down the hall, knocking on doors. No answer, no answer. End of the hall, door opens. *What are you doing?*

Physics homework, he answers.

His name is Leonard, I don't know him all that well, and I ask *can you come downtown with me? Please, it's important.* My voice holds the urgency. If he doesn't say yes, I'll be reaching the point of panic. It's Philadelphia, it's already late, after nine, not safe to travel alone especially being female—I hate that—and stores are closing soon, I don't know what time, and I need that song tonight.

Sure.

Deep breath.

En route I tell Leonard what happened. It's maybe the first time he's heard any of it. We're fringe friends, mostly. Dorm friends in common, maybe a couple of one-on-one conversations. Now he tells me about his last girlfriend, about the woman he likes now. It's beginning to drizzle and it feels strangely, poetically, appropriate.

The first store doesn't have the album, the next is closed. Another *no* after that. In each place I buy something, Shawn Colvin on sale, Dar Williams for $18.99. New musicians for me, never heard them live. I get Dar's CD in Giovanni's Room, the gay and lesbian bookstore around Fourteenth and Pine, first time I've been brave enough to go inside.

I'm giving up on finding *Sure Thing,* but Leonard wants to make one more stop. He wants a particular fitted baseball cap and he thinks there's a store nearby which might have it. We walk another two blocks to the hat store but it's locked. Grates are covering the windows. I peer through and pull the door handle anyway. Leonard points out the hat he wants and says he'll come back later in the week. Then he notices we're right next to this used CD place. I say, *what the hell,* and we go in. *Sure Thing* is there.

The song is on an album called *Relentless* by Michelle Malone and Drag the River, $7.99 plus tax. The cover is brown and yellow and turquoise. I read the lyrics then listen through once

MAP   99

while Leonard browses at the far end of the store, then pay the cashier. It's still raining outside.

Waiting for the bus, we run into two dorm acquaintances—a couple—and decide to share a cab. I'm silent on the drive, focusing on the cross hanging from the rear-view mirror, a cab driver whose face I haven't seen, who's probably fundamentalist of some sort and thus homophobic, because who else hangs crosses in their cab. Is it paranoia or street smarts to not mention Catrina, to stay quiet until my feet are safely on brick? Even if he wasn't homophobic, just surprised, his hands could slip on the steering wheel, swerve us into another car as he turned to see who this dyke was in the back of his cab. Nineteen flights up again this fear, something else in control of my life, an elevator can stop mid-floor, something else keeping me from my destination. Someday I will live a safe walk from everywhere, one flight up.

Now on the nineteenth floor it's me lying on my bed again, lyrics in front of me, *Sure Thing* on repeat, West Philly sirens in the background, and the choking sobs finally come.

And if I'm falling down, please don't let me know, and if I come undone, I'll try not to let it show, I am working on a sure thing.

I let the tears sting my eyes, soak my face, let the mucus build up and drip dampness onto my pillow, my sheets, my shirt. I gasp for breath as the reality shakes me to my core.

After a while my crying slows and I pick up the mix from Catrina again. With the song playing I can read a little more slowly and there it is, the song is on the mix after all, small cursive in the middle of side B, and I don't know what to do with that fact, with anything. I pick up the phone, get machine after machine. It's 11:36. I email Matthew. *It's too much to tell over email. Call me please. Whatever time it is, 4 AM or whatever. Heartbreak too much to go alone....*

I reread Catrina's email. All I can do is dissect her words. *I can only love you as a friend.* She said *can,* not *do.* Somehow that's comforting. The love is still there. A relationship not working out is something I can grasp. Feelings changing is something I can't.

Catrina's words will resonate differently in later years as part of the cliche of phrases we use as crutches in endings: true and hurtful and kind and wrong, words that take the place of what we don't understand about ourselves and what we're not willing to give and what we're still afraid of. *I can't do this anymore,* I will tell someone, aching as I pull away. *I do love you, you know,* someone else will say to me, just before she drives off. And again, and again, I will be left in this place of brokenness, gathering shards of what was good and slivers of hope. I will discover, here, something I love about myself: a determined faith in the potential of every human being, an unshakable belief that it is always possible to grow. And although I will also discover here disappointment, each time those I love choose the fear over the growth, and although I will learn to draw boundaries and shut doors and say goodbyes, I will not give up on Possibility, on hope, on love.

I press *r* to reply. *Dear Catrina,* I type. Then I run out of words, and I, too, turn to song lyrics to name my feelings. I type Catrina lyrics by Fred Small that I had once wished for Jake to sing to me.

Wherever the light before you leads you, and whether you find me or no, my love will travel softly at your shoulder, and abide by you wherever you may go. Go your way I cannot hold you, nor would I

MAP   101

detain you if I could, I will wait for you in the clearing, on the other side of the wood.

My own words are returning. It is time to begin letting go, but not without a proper *fare thee well.* I write to Catrina, *I think it's important for the both of us that I do come on Thursday...all I ask is that little bit of time for us to be together, in whatever form together means for us that day. Carpe diem and no talk of the future. You can have forever for yourself.*

Something incredible got us this far, something that is the basis for the deep friendship I hope we will continue to have....I love you, and unless you ask not to hear it I am going to continue telling you that. The definition changes but the words remain true.

It's 2:28 AM. *Sure Thing* is still playing. I hit the *send* button.

A Freshman Dork Named Jake

It's messed up but in the morning the one person I want to talk to is Jake. When Matthew calls, he says *yeah that's messed up, but in some warped way, it also makes sense,* and he gives me Jake's new phone number. Although I've only heard from Jake once directly in the last year and half, Matthew's been a kind of go-between, delivering regards and occasional updates. So I know that Jake transferred schools, wants to be a rabbi, and has been dating someone for over a year who Matthew thinks is a good match for him.

Jake knows about Catrina, right? I ask.

Yeah, Matthew says.

Good, I say. I'm glad Jake knows. I'm glad because I don't have to come out to him in order to have this conversation, and because it feels like he's still some vague part of my life even though we haven't spoken for so long.

Jake's not in when I call, so I leave a message and hope he'll call back. Restless, wanting to ask what's on my mind, I start writing him an email, but I don't send it.

I'm staring at the ceiling when Tyler calls. I remind myself not to mention Catrina, to focus on Tyler's roommate crisis.

MAP   103

But it turns out Catrina has told Tyler what happened, in case I needed someone to talk to.

Are you okay? Tyler asks.

I guess so. I'll tell her more after I find out if *she's* okay. *Did you talk to your roommate?*

Yeah. She says she guessed a long time ago, she was just waiting for me to say something.

So she's cool with it all? I feel a layer of tension relax in my shoulders.

Oh yeah. And my brother keeps making jokes about am I going to take Heather to sorority date parties, so I think he knows, too. Now I just have to tell my best friend.

We strategize about that. Tyler's voice says as much as her words. She sounds jazzed by this last telling, not really nervous about the next one, just wanting to be sure her best friend hears it firsthand. My friend Tyler is an amazing human being, I realize, not for the first time.

Tyler asks if she can read her best friend a piece of my writing called *Fluid Sexuality*. It's a dialogue I wrote a year and half ago, inspired by *The Incredibly True Adventures of Two Girls in Love*, where one character tries to explain to another that she's looking for a soulmate, not a gender. I showed the piece to Tyler when she came over for dinner, and I've been meaning to revise it and then maybe submit it somewhere. It's not really polished enough yet to show lots of people. But Tyler wants to use it in coming out to her best friend—how can I say no? I'm honored and glad that my writing can help in this way.

I'll send it to you right now, I say, opening folders on my Powerbook until I locate the file. I add a copyright notice and my name and send it off before I can change my mind. Then we talk for a while about what just happened with me and Catrina.

Are you still going to Washington? Tyler asks.

I think so. Do you mind being my contact, in case something happens and my parents need to reach me? I don't really want to have to explain all this.

Of course, says Tyler.

Remembering AJ's invitation to the movies, when I get off the phone I put on my jester cap and overalls, comfort clothes, and take the elevator down to the High Rise courtyard. I'm early, way early. I wait for AJ and her friends under the dueling tampons, the sculpture big and red and looming.

It's Sunday when Catrina writes back. *You are so incredibly wonderful,* she says, but it's still over and she doesn't want to see me next week. I'm too hurt and numb to be angry at this new proclamation. *Maybe over the summer,* she says. Today is Groundhog Day. February. The summer's a long way off.

Jake returns my call.

I'm feeling deja vu, I tell him. *Only I'm on the other side and I think you might have some insight. I've been wanting to talk to you for a while anyway, about us....what was or wasn't and how and why it all happened the way it did. Do you remember the Indigo Girls song, "Language or the Kiss?"*

Yes, he says.

It's been theming through my head for the last year and a half, I say. *It's been my greatest fear since ending things with you that I could never have both writing and a relationship, that I would have to make the choice. And then I found Catrina.*

MAP 105

I'm not sure how to continue the conversation at this point, so I wind up reading him part of the email that I didn't send.

Jake, me and you were never meant to be a forever thing, but under different circumstances I think we could have had a good relationship for a while. We met at the wrong time. I was still trying to figure out about me and writing, its role in my life, and I couldn't do that while being in a relationship. I needed to be completely self-absorbed to figure it out. And if I had tried to have both the writing and you then, I would have just wound up resenting you because the emotional involvement would have taken away from my writing.

I pause for air and make sure I can still hear Jake breathing on the other end before continuing. *I was scared of losing control. I had no choice but to push you away if I wanted to follow my dream. And I did try to leave an out, by saying talk to me in September. I did mean that. I know by then you were involved with someone else. Did you try to wait? Were you really planning to talk to me then? Did you ultimately come to the realization that I wasn't going to be the one, and thus you shouldn't hang around waiting? If you had thought I was the one, or could have been, what would you have done?*

Reading aloud words which are so new and uncrafted is a peculiar sensation. I float in and out of the meaning, trying to both be part of what I'm saying and read it without stumbling. *Catrina showed me that I could have both,* I continue, *writing and a relationship, that I wouldn't have to make the choice. But that wouldn't have been able to happen if I hadn't gone through everything with you, if I hadn't made the choice and taken that time to devote completely to myself and my own dreams, to be secure in them. And now Catrina's at that very point, with forty thousand dollars of loans to pay off, no job, not knowing what she wants to do that can earn her money and needing the space to figure it out alone.*

Thank you, Jake says when I'm done. There's a pause as I take in these unexpected words. *I know that probably isn't what you're looking to hear, but thank you. I was thinking all this time I hadn't meant anything to you.*

I guess I'd tried to create that impression, I say. *I didn't know how to deal with my feelings.* I almost tell him about the story I wrote right after I called it off, where his character was in someone else's bed the next week and mine was left brooding, alone and angry at her art for depriving her of joy.

Jake tells me about the rebound relationship he got into right after me, and I realize how close to the mark I was.

Don't get into a rebound relationship, he advises me. *I just got more depressed about you afterwards. I barely even thought about her. I still feel rotten about that.*

He's being open and it's a comfortable conversation, and he then says something which kind of surprises me, but feels right. *We were too brief. We couldn't have lasted, but we were too brief.*

Yeah, we were too brief, I say, then ask, *why do you think we couldn't have lasted?*

He says that I would've eventually needed to break it off to explore my sexuality.

We talk about us. We talk about what happened the night we hooked up. What I remember is him initiating it, kissing me first. *You were the one who pulled me down,* Jake says. *I would have been happy holding your hand all night.*

I'm glad he told me that.

And then Jake talks about his girlfriend, how they got together early in that September, totally clicked. And I wonder briefly *what*

MAP   107

if he hadn't met her, what could Jake and I have been? not sure if it's aimless wondering or regret, but it doesn't really matter now. Because what I'm feeling now is closure. The closure I'm not getting with Catrina, I *am* getting with Jake. Even though we never used the term boyfriend when we were together, it finally feels like he's an ex, like we had a legitimate relationship.

Why hadn't it felt like a legitimate relationship before? I know the answer as soon as I ask myself the question. It hadn't because only meeting and our first date and hooking up occurred in person. The rest took place through email and a couple of letters. I hadn't understood back then that the realness of feelings isn't dependent on the medium.

As Jake and I keep talking, and I hear more about what Jake's doing now and how he's really gotten his life together in a way I totally respect and admire—passionate about his classes, focused, driven—and as he tells me about this sunrise drive I should take up the Washington coast, about how beautiful it is out there and he hopes I'll still make the trip, I realize I love him. Not one of those kinds of love that needs a clarifier: *as a friend, as family, someone to spend my life with*. It's just Jake.

What It Is to Lose a Zoe

Morning again. I'm worn out, calmer, settling, but empty inside. Physical empty, since I've barely eaten for three days.

The emptiness focuses me. What's Important: Food. People. Family. Breathing. *Family.* I think about Zoe, the baby Catrina and I were going to have together. In my mind she is a newborn nursing at Catrina's breast while I look on with wonder. A toddler, holding my hand as she takes her first steps. A kindergartener, riding a tricycle, learning to read. Zoe, there when I need love, interrupting me when she needs love back. *There's not going to be any Zoe.* I close my eyes, feel the blow of this realization, know this is the final blow. Know I need food in my stomach to deal with it.

I open my fridge. Empty. Cabinets, empty too. My body is becoming jittery.

I go down the hall, knock on the door of a friend I haven't seen all week, *do you have anything I can eat?* He gives me what he has, an apple and a granola bar. The jitteriness slows as soon as the food is in my hands, and then I realize that there's someone else who can help me too. She's on the other side of the campus, 34th and Walnut in Bennett Hall, and miraculously her weekly office hour is right now and the apple and granola bar I

MAP   109

eat slowly are just enough to get me to her. *Her* being Professor Snow.

During one of the first conversations we had in her office, Professor Snow fed me couscous. None of my other professors had ever done anything like that, and the simple kindness made me feel at home. I go to see Professor Snow now because of that couscous. Somehow I know she'll understand what it is to lose a Zoe.

When I get to Professor Snow's office, someone else is in there. I'm fidgety out in the hall—like a Tourette's attack triggered by waiting—and then a classmate shows up and sits down and talks to me, and that's what gets me through the next ten minutes. And then we both go in to Professor Snow's office together, and the fidgety slows and I start choking up and I tell them about Zoe and everything that's happened since our last class and they're like family for me, listening, caring.

They listen and they soothe, and I'm not conscious of exactly what they're saying, only that it's working, it's calming me. After I'm calmer, we talk about my classmate's story, which brings me back into the world of other people a little, that feeling of three. That comfortable feeling I had growing up with Mom and Dad where you know you're cared for and you don't even have to say a word. And after a little while I even participate, and then the conversation winds to a natural close and there are other people waiting in the hall, so we start standing up.

As my classmate is gathering her things, Professor Snow says to me, *I don't have anything to give you. I want to give you something.*

She's looking around her office and digging around her purse and finally she pulls out a honey-lemon cough drop and says *it's all I have but it's something.* And then she gives me a huge hug, and I'm crying, and it's the first time anyone's touched me or I've touched anyone since all this happened. Somehow I was too afraid to relax around anyone else.

I go out with honey lemon in my mouth and walk my way downtown.

I'm not exactly sure where I'm heading, somewhere quiet. I go slow over the river, concentrate on the motion of my feet on the bridge, my fingertips touching the guardrail. I cross the bridge and follow the pavement alongside Rittenhouse Square. I know when I get to Borders that this is where I was heading. The light's streaming in beautifully through the windows of the cafe upstairs. I go to the notebook and journal section first. I can always tell when I've got the right notebook. I write differently in it, better or more from the heart or something. The one I find this time is more expensive than any I've ever let myself get before. It's brown paper bag color and solid spiral and wooden cover with a coffee mug cut out. I get tea and go by the window in the cafe, it's so bright out, and I cry my eyes out and write this letter to Zoe. I write her all about her mom and me, and I bring Zoe alive just long enough to say goodbye.

I walk back feeling like I'm whole again, like I've just finished reading the greatest book of my life and had the big cry at the end, and I'm whole and stronger for the reading. And as the book closes I come to realize what it is about fiction that so appeals to me. There is something in its possibilities and its closure that is rare to ever find in real life.

I feel like I've experienced a merging of fiction and real life with Catrina. It's not something that could last. It's a state that would be unhealthy for a long relationship, where you need to be able to change and adapt and compromise and entertain

MAP   111

messiness and trade in dreams for plans and goals and pay-
checks. But for this brief moment, it is the most amazing wonderful thing in the world.

When I get home, I take my favorite photo of Catrina and
place it in Zoe's book, and then place the whole thing in a box
with old journals for safekeeping. I wonder if I'll ever show it to
anyone else.

That evening I book reservations at the youth hostel and
make alternate plans with Sasha since Catrina won't be driving
me down to Oregon. I send Tyler my itinerary and emergency
contact information. Then I read through some of the emails
from a few weeks back. I find myself crying, missing Catrina,
and then reaching for the phone.

The last contact I've had with Catrina was over email, and
it didn't feel like contact, not the way it had when it was only
email that we were using to communicate. Now it has the feel of
retreat, of wimping out, of avoidance. And despite how emphati-
cally she said she didn't want to see me, I know from myself
how much *could* have happened for her in these three days. It's
like when you're driving, the road isn't static. Every second it's a
different road, and who can say what will come next?

Dialing reminds me of the first time I called and I hesitate—
what if I just don't? what if I just leave it like this?—and then press
the last digit.

Catrina's flipping channels, describing what's on the sta-
tions, interrupting to tell her roommate something. It seems as
though she's only half-paying attention to me as we talk.

I ask her, nervous, about the emails. Once we had planned
to publish the first 209 emails we'd written each other—a lurid
bestseller to pay off her college loans—but now they're the only

thing left, and I elicit a promise, *this is just between us*. I don't want someone else reading, prescribing their own meaning onto the words. Because it's the meaning we gave them, gave the rhythm of them, that created the response in our own hearts, as much as the words themselves.

Yes, that is just between us, she says, *and it will be something we will always have, and share.* And I wonder, can I believe her? Will I keep my own promise?

As I write in the coming years about our relationship, fabricating new words, evoking old meanings, losing track of the origins of particular sentences, I will think often about this promise and what it means to keep it. I will make my choices with care. I will keep more of my promise than my readers may imagine, and less than Catrina might have hoped. I will live with this knowledge.

Catrina makes getting-off-the-phone noises and I look at the clock. We've been talking for forty minutes, but it doesn't feel that way. I end the conversation, *I love you.* She says *me too,* and I don't know if she's distracted or if she really doesn't feel it anymore.

Lay Your Finger Anywhere Down

The plane lands in Seattle on Thursday evening. I call Tyler to say I got in safely. *Are you going to try to see Catrina while you're out there?* Tyler asks.

No. Although I've thought about it. I left Catrina's address back in Philly so I wouldn't be tempted to show up at her doorstep. I don't want our first meeting to be full of disappointment.

Just so you know, Tyler says, *she emailed me this morning thinking you might and asking me to talk you out of it.* In my memory of this conversation, I won't remember if I felt hurt by this news, or if I suppressed anger, or if I just cataloged it away somewhere. Perhaps I was simply too distracted by airport bustle and new surroundings for feeling to register, or perhaps I already understood that this trip was now my own adventure. *I told her you were my friend and I wouldn't do that,* says Tyler, *but it doesn't sound like it would be a pleasant experience.*

Once I hang up from Tyler, I head outside. It's a little warmer than Philly. I've got my hiking boots and backpack, feel like a traveler—a good feeling. I'm on the west coast for the first time ever and the next three days are mine. No expectations, just whatever comes. If I want, I can explore. If I want to sleep the days away, walk the city depressed and lonesome for three days, I can do that too, but I don't think I will.

A guy dressed like I am, boots and backpack, shorts though, is waiting for the same bus, and we start to talk. I say I want to go down to the Pacific Ocean, I've never seen it before, and when the bus stops near the youth hostel, he gets off with me and we wander down to the harbor. It's dark out and we watch the boats and the water with easy conversation and peaceful silence. As I flew over the center of the continent, I could feel the claustrophobia of land on all four sides. A sense that I would long for the ocean if I didn't live nearby. I watch the reflection of the dock lights in the water, the dark edge of horizon. I'm here. This is me. I can remember feeling this way before, free and new and ready for something else to come along. No one out here knows my story. I can recreate myself in possibility.

It's a different *new*, though, than starting high school or college or camp or my semester in Israel. I've completed a journey. I'm not trying to reinvent myself into someone better or different or flawless. I'm not trying to hide confusion or nosepicking or inexperience. I'm not scared anymore that no one will ever love me, that no one will ever find me beautiful, that I'll reveal the wrong thing about myself and discover the elementary-school-style cruelties of everybody else. I just *am*. I can feel the weight lifted off me.

As I meander through the city in the wee hours of sunrise, feeling settles into fact: I was in love with a woman. She is part of my history. If tomorrow I were to marry Jake or my fellow backpacked traveler or some guy crossing the street, it would still be a part of me. I loved a woman. I loved Catrina.

MAP   115

It seals my place, it marks my passage. It is a starred city on the map of my life.

Will our eyes ever meet? I wonder.

I read the yellow pages in the youth hostel where I'm staying, smile at travelers and clerks and people on the street. People are friendly here, smiling back, chit-chatting at cash registers. I visit a temp agency, a branch of Seafirst bank, the inviting wood rooms of Elliot Bay Books. I eat lunch in a cafe that feels like it's been waiting for me. I elevate to the top of the Space Needle and circle around, considering neighborhoods. My body is still on East Coast time, so I've done all this and it's barely three o'clock. I walk and walk, meandering through little shops, exploring side streets, soaking in the energy of this city, and eventually I make my way down to the bus station just in time to meet Sasha.

Sasha's shaved her head and it's just starting to grow back in. She's here only overnight, she's signed up for studio time in Oregon tomorrow afternoon. We go to Capitol Hill, where we eat dinner at a Thai restaurant and then walk arm-in-arm down the main drag, checking out the stores and the people. The name of this area is funny to me, because when I hear *Capitol Hill*, I think of Washington D.C. and lots of stone white buildings and people in suits. This is more like Greenwich Village or Philly's South Street, tattoos and colorful clothing, artists and street people and students. It's so wonderful to be with Sasha in this new place.

Hey Sasha, I say, grinning at her, *ask me if I'm a tree.*

She grins back. *Are you a tree?*

I say *no,* and she gives me a one-armed hug and says *I'm glad you're here.* Then we both turn to watch a woman pass by with a tiny dog poking out of her knapsack. Another woman passes by on a bicycle, short hair, a pink triangle sticker stuck to her helmet.

There are rainbow flags hanging from the lightposts, and I wonder, *what if I run into her? What if I just happen to run into Catrina?* The odds are probably small since she lives in Olympia, but she's been coming to Seattle to look for jobs and I know she likes Capitol Hill. *Would I even recognize her?* The thoughts won't leave my head, and I realize I *don't* want to run into Catrina. I want this to be *my* city.

I told my parents I wouldn't call while I was out here. I didn't say *I'm not staying at Catrina's after all,* I just used some line about me needing to do this trip independently, figure out my future on my own, *call Tyler in case of emergency.* I haven't told them about Catrina, the falling in love part, although I know Mom senses it. The irony is that's the part I most wanted to tell. But the way everything came out, the way Mom coaxed it out of me on the phone that day, I wasn't prepared, and now how can I say *we broke up* when Mom will just interrogate me, *how can you break up if you've never met?* So here I am. I've walked nearly the whole city today, I'm making it mine.

Back at the hostel, Sasha goes to sleep, and I use the pay phones in the hall to call a couple of people from the Indigo Girls list who live in the area and try to make plans. This woman Whitney and I hit it off. We talk for a couple of hours until I've got to go to the bathroom so badly it hurts, and we agree to meet up the next afternoon. So after Sasha leaves, Whitney and I hang out. She's a few years older, finishing grad school, an

MAP 117

amazing guitar player. We spend some time just relaxing and talking in her apartment, and then she drives me all over the city to the parts I haven't seen, the parts it's better to have a car for, and it's really beautiful. There are mountains in the distance, Puget Sound below, picturesque little houses, expansive sunset and sweet breeze like another voice weaving into our conversation.

We hadn't really emailed before, so I was a little surprised when Whitney responded to my post asking for suggestions of what to see and do in Seattle, more surprised when she included her phone number. I'm not really sure what made me call. But I'm so glad I did. She's easy to talk to. She's fun. She's intelligent. She's got pictures of hot women decorating her computer and she sighs as she tells the story of being hit on in a bar by Amy Ray of the Indigo Girls back before Whitney realized she was a lesbian.

I crash at Whitney's place for a couple of nights and get to meet a bunch of people from the list. We eat burgers at a mountainside diner. We play guitar. We go *en masse* to a Seattle Reign basketball game and cheer for number three, Kate Paye, Whitney's latest crush. We watch *Thelma and Louise* and *Fried Green Tomatoes*.

It's the first time I've hung out in a group of women-who-love-women, and I want to do it more. There's an energy I've never felt before. Maybe it's the feeling that we're self-contained, that nothing's missing. Whenever else I've been in a group of women, the topic of conversation would eventually turn to guys. Here, it's about us.

It hasn't rained once since I've been here, and I take that to be a sign.

I'm definitely moving out here this summer, I announce to my new friends.

When it's just the two of us, Whitney and I swap relationship stories. She's met Catrina a couple of times. I keep coming back to that, wanting to ask questions but at the same time not wanting to. What would I ask, *what's she like?*

She tells me, though. *We were at that shindigo last fall*—a gathering of Seattle-area people from the Indigo Girls Mailing List—*and Catrina was so rude,* Whitney says. *I tried to engage her in conversation and she completely blew me off.*

I don't want to believe what Whitney is saying, though she sounds truthful. I don't like feeling as if I have to choose between Whitney's perception of Catrina and my own. I try to reconcile this new information with the Catrina I knew. I recall Catrina telling me once about her public persona, one that shows up in crowds because she gets uncomfortable and nervous and that demands to be the center of attention at parties. I decide that if Whitney and Catrina had met one-on-one, Whitney would probably have a better impression.

Whitney doesn't like Catrina at all, seems surprised that I did, do, can't see us together. *You're way too cute and creatively intellectual for her,* Whitney says, which makes me blush.

It's good to be able to tell the story from the beginning to the end and to hear Whitney respond. I like that Whitney is older, more experienced, able to play mentor, but still regards me as an equal.

Whitney's all angry at how Catrina treated me. *She kept the Dar Williams tickets?* Whitney's eyebrows go up. *That's bullshit.*

I told her to keep them and take a friend, I say.

She should at least pay you back for them.

MAP   119

I shrug. *Whatever. She doesn't have the money.*

You're too nice, Whitney says. *She could have sold them and paid you back.*

Whitney goes on about Catrina's treatment of me, taking on that anger, anger that I can't feel.

I would have bought the tickets off her, Whitney says later. *I tried to get tickets for that show but they were sold out. I could have bought the tickets off her and then me and you could have gone.*

We would have had to miss the Seattle Reign game, I point out.

I forgot about that. Whitney holds up one palm, then the other. *Dar. Kate Paye. Maybe it's better we didn't have to make that choice.*

As Whitney drives me to the airport, then comes in to wait until my plane arrives, I catch myself wondering, not for the first time, *what if the situation were different?* She's rather cute and creatively intellectual herself. Dressed casual but confident in a henley sweater and jeans, hands in her back pockets, her short hair brushes into her face as she discusses photography and her master's program in communications. She meets me in a solid hug before I board the 737. *What if I was interested in something happening rather than cautiously keeping my guard up?*

You Still Haven't Kissed a Girl?

When I go back to Philly, Whitney and I keep emailing and calling. Every so often she sends me information about apartments or jobs. *You still haven't kissed a girl?* she says one time. *You have to. Like this week.* There's an Indigo Girls concert coming up, and Whitney jokes about buying a ticket and coming East so she can be the first girl I kiss. Part of me wishes she would. I tell her about AJ, who I'm still attracted to, and she tells me *don't go for a straight girl,* but when I say AJ's leaving for Australia pretty soon, she tells me *go for it.*

I'm settling back into being single. It's comfortable and familiar and I like the inward-focus, the space for uninterrupted thought. I'm not feeling the waves of loneliness that used to wash over me every so often before Catrina, the fear of being alone forever. Maybe that's gone for good. But now I have all this floating lust and attraction. It stops on every beautiful person I see, and I wish I were a different kind of person, a person who could be attracted to someone one minute and kissing them the next and not stuck in messy aftermath for years after the fact.

I'm realizing how much unacknowledged sexual tension there is in my friendships. The tension of never saying *I like you.*

MAP   121

The tension of never saying *I'm attracted* or *I want you to go out with me*. The tension of always assuming it's unrequited love or lust or attraction but never asking.

I embark on a quest of sorts, attempting to turn some of that tension into sexual honesty—the truthful expression of my feelings. I try to say things like *you're hot* or *I liked you way back when*. The boy I liked at the beginning of freshman year says to me, *I'm flattered*. Not *I liked you too*, but *I'm flattered*, and it strikes me that this is the perfect answer, respectful and honest and not putting forth nonexistent feelings or shying away from mine.

For Valentine's Day I send Tyler an email telling her how special she is, how much I admire her, how much the night we met—when I thought she was straight—I wanted to hold her hand, how glad I am we're friends. She writes back *I'm glad we're friends too, you're kinda like the big sister I never had, or something*, and I feel like she's found the perfect words to describe us.

I keep ruminating on attraction and relationships, exploring the nuances in a way I hadn't been able to before. Our culture relies so much on *terms*—sex, boyfriend, date, hooking up—and if it isn't a clearcut *will you go out with me?* and nothing physical happens—*physical* meaning at least a kiss—it doesn't count. But that leaves out so much, and it puts the weight in the wrong places. Why should a messed up one-night-stand count more than a summer of eye contact and deep conversation? Why should hooking up with Jake weigh more than the conversations and emails where we revealed feelings? I decide I want to value my feelings more, but I can't seem to shrink the importance of the terminology. Maybe because the terminology is the short-hand we use to communicate our experience, the way grades stand in for education, and it's too entrenched in our world to escape easily. Or maybe just because I've been measuring myself against it for so long, and I still don't quite measure up.

The next time AJ and I hang out, I tell her, *I wanted to ask you out that first time at Chats. I would have, if you'd given any sign that you were into women.*
    Did you think I was? she asks.
    Interested in women?
    She nods. I tell her what Matthew told me about listening to too much folk music to be straight. I was pissed when he first said that, because it's a stereotype, but now I think it makes sense. People who listen to folk music *do* tend to be open-minded, and if you think of sexuality on a continuum, being open to the possibility would probably impact the experiences of the people in the middle part of that spectrum.
    AJ laughs. *Yeah, I do listen to a lot of folk music.* Then she pauses, considers the question. *It's not that I'm averse to the idea,* she says. *I just don't think a woman would do it for me, you know?*
    I nod. *Fair enough.*
    What about you? she asks. *Are you more interested in girls or guys now?*
    I don't know, I answer.
    That's cool, AJ says. Then she grins. *So are you going to let me give you a makeover next week, for my goodbye party?*

    I don't know if it's the conversation which makes me say yes, or that I trust AJ, or just the fact that I'm attracted to her. *Why am I so nervous about a makeover?* I arrive at AJ's an hour before the party's supposed to start. I'm terrified, but also excited and really kind of curious.

MAP 123

I sit on AJ's bed and she kneels in front of me, covering each of my zits with foundation.

Hold still, she says. I try to hold still, try to relax, but the whole time she's so close. It would be so easy just to lean forward and kiss her. What if I asked her, a friend favor, if I said to her *Whitney dared me to kiss a girl this week?*

I hold back. I'd just be more confused if I did it that way, hurt if she said no. She's so close, though. She takes off my glasses and begins applying mascara to my eyelashes. I flinch.

Hold still, AJ says. *I promise I won't get it in your eye.*

Sorry, I say, trying to smile and breathe and not show her how freaked out I am to have this stuff on my eyelashes, even though I'm only letting her near my eyes because she already knows and understands. She's gentle, and then she's done with my eyes and she's applying more foundation and showing me how to blot lipstick.

Can I look? I ask.

Almost, she says. She adds a little more blush to my left cheek. Then she steps back and looks at me, and shakes her head up and down approvingly. *Yeah.*

It's overdone. AJ puts on her own makeup and hers seems a little overdone too, but not as much as mine. I don't look like me. The lipstick is dark, a dark maroon sort of color that seems a little hooker-ish, a little costume-ish. The foundation covers my zits nicely, which is a plus, but it feels caked on. The eyes also seem over-the-top, dark and fake and enhancing the hooker effect.

I don't feel like me. I wouldn't want to look like this on a regular basis. But it's not so terrifying now that it's on. It's just a costume. A costume that fits funny because I don't know how to act in it, how to act sexual in a feminine way. It's a uniform for a game that AJ knows how to play and I think I'm beyond learning.

As I stare into the mirror, I can see that with a little less on the eyes, a closer-to-lip-color lipstick, I might actually look sort of like myself. If this didn't take time, if it didn't look pasty, I could see using makeup to cover up my zits. But I'm still glad a half hour later when AJ's roommate breaks out his face-painting kit and coaxes me into letting him paint balloons on my cheeks, a more comfortable and recognizable costume layered on top of the one AJ's given me.

That's Where It Happened

I go back home for spring break. In the car with my dad on the way from the train station to my house, I ask, *Is Mom going to keep grilling me about the trip and Catrina? Because I really really don't want her to.*

I don't think so, he says.

Good, I say. *Um, Catrina and I were kind of involved, as much as you can be involved over the phone and email, and it didn't end so happily, and I still don't feel much like talking about it, but some day I'll tell you more.*

It's easy to say this to Dad because he doesn't ask questions like Mom does. Mom actually asked flat out *did you stay with Catrina all four nights?* when I called to let my parents know I was back in Philly. I told her that the plans had gotten a little changed, *don't worry about it, I was safe, I know how to take care of myself.* Knowing that if I answered her first question, there would be a dozen more to follow.

Over Shabbat dinner I tell my parents about Seattle. Mom is impressed that I checked out the web temp agency. Dad says, half-joking, *so you're actually planning to be employed when you graduate?*

Maybe, I say, noncommittal. I haven't quite given up on making the bestseller list first, although I haven't touched my novel-in-progress in months and months. Mom and Dad exchange looks, still not trusting that I *do* understand that they aren't supporting me anymore once I get that diploma.

Did you take pictures? Mom asks.

I tell her I didn't bring my camera, and she's disappointed. *Next time,* I say.

My parents seem resigned to me moving to Seattle. They talk about visiting me, maybe renting a place for a few weeks.

I tell my parents about the public transportation, how you can fasten your bike to the back of the bus to travel across town, how Greyhound makes it easy to travel to Oregon and Vancouver, and then I accidentally let slip something about staying with Sasha in a youth hostel.

I thought you were staying with Catrina, says Mom.

Uh oh. I can't go there. I just can't. *Please don't ask, Mom.* I try to say it as nicely as possible, but firmly. *Be glad of what I do share.*

She looks hurt. *It's time to clean the table.* But she doesn't pursue it this time.

After dinner I unpack. It's strange to put my Powerbook on my desk and see the scene where I fell in love and have it not feel that way anymore. It's strange to look at a desk and think to myself *that's where it happened.* And to go in the basement thinking *this is where we spoke for the first time* and realize Catrina would never recognize it.

Mom says some things are *beshert,* a Yiddish word, *destined, meant to be, happen for a reason.* Maybe I just needed Catrina for that little bit of time I had her, just long enough to love and be loved. Just long enough to learn that *alone* didn't have to be

MAP   127

my fate, as we wished away the space between the coasts until, briefly, it was just the two of us, together.

I go online after my parents are asleep and reread all our beginning emails. My email account saved copies of the ones I sent along with the ones Catrina sent me, so in a way it's like reliving the whole thing. But I pick up on things like typos I hadn't noticed before, and it feels different. Halfway through I start crying, wanting that beginning back, and then when I get up to go to the bathroom, the feelings seem so far away. I'm in my parents' house with the snow melted and my Pooh bear next to my pillow and the smell of fresh-baked *challah* downstairs. I can hear the clock chiming in the next room and see the lights from across the street. There's a photo essay I created a few years ago sitting on my shelf waiting to be reexamined, next to all the books I've loved since childhood, and Catrina seems so remote and unimportant right now. Even rereading the emails, the magic is gone, the emotions are beginning to fade.

I Vow I'll Make It Up To Her Somehow

Tyler gets three tickets to the Indigo Girls show on the last night of vacation—for me, her, and Heather—and finds us all a place to crash because the show is at Hofstra University in New York. The three of us meet up outside Tyler's dorm and walk the few more blocks to Thirtieth Street Station. It's the first time I've seen Tyler and Heather together since the night we all met in person.

Tyler plays with some little kids on the train, and Heather just watches, tells me she doesn't really like kids. Tyler's good with them, grinning and cute and asking them questions and letting them climb all over her. I take a few photographs of them, then I watch Heather through the camera lens, searching for how she sees Tyler. I notice that Tyler and Heather haven't really been touching at all. They seem more like friends than a couple. I wonder about that, whether it's being in public or around me or just the way they are. I think about Tyler and sex, a thought that hasn't come before, about how Heather knows Tyler in a way I never will but does she know how gentle to be? Does anyone realize the way I do how special Tyler is?

I've been thinking more about what Tyler said to me on Valentine's Day, *you're like the big sister I never had.* Thinking about this way to love someone.

MAP   129

The summer I was seventeen, I had a counselor, Cory, who I adopted as a big brother. He was hot and I liked him and I knew he was twenty-six and I was seventeen, so big brother was a kind of relationship I could allow myself, where I would be able to love him and care and want to get close without developing a romantic crush and running into *camper-counselor relationships aren't permitted* or *you're too young for me anyway* or *I'm not attracted to you.* Big brother was an artifice but maybe it was the right one. He'd play guitar in his room, and I'd sit on the other bed across from him, sometimes singing with him, sometimes talking, sometimes just listening as he sang. Sometimes both of us quiet except for the guitar. And the eye contact. Meaningful without words, just connection I guess. It made me not afraid of eyes, made me want that, made me trust him and start to trust other people to be good like that too. Two years later the tutor came and took it all away, making eye contact with me in a tutoring session and then turning it into something dangerous. But the summer I was seventeen, I had Cory. I opened up to Cory, sharing my fears and questions and thoughts, and he listened and answered and met my eyes and strummed gently.

I remember leaving at the end of the summer, at the security gate at the airport, going back to Cory four times for hugs, big ones, long ones. On the third one I got the guts to say *I love you* and he said back *you're a great kid.* On the fourth one I said *good luck with Shira,* because we all thought he and our counselor Shira were dating and not telling us. I don't remember what he said back—maybe he said *thanks,* maybe they weren't dating at all and he was confused and said *what* and I repeated it—but I remember it took lots of guts to say it, guts to mention it at all and guts to mean it, and then I couldn't go back for another hug after that and I still didn't know if he loved me.

I told Tyler on Valentine's Day how I felt about her, but I still feel like I left something out. The depth. Maybe I don't say it because I'm not sure if the feeling runs this deep both ways, or maybe because I sense that just saying it will change her somehow. I want this part of Tyler to stay this way, beautiful and untouched.

That night Tyler and Heather sit together on the couch, Tyler's head resting in Heather's lap. It's chaste enough that they could still just be friends but it's tender. I'm grateful to see that. I feel like I'd do anything to keep Tyler from getting hurt, ever, but I know I can't keep her safe.

What I don't know, won't begin to understand until much later, as I am writing Tyler alive in the pages of my memoir and losing my need for her continued presence in my life, is the ephemeral nature of our connection. I'll feel guilty, then, for not needing her, for letting an email sit lost for months without responding, for neglecting the friendship. I'll wonder at the nature of feelings themselves, how someone can be so important for a season and then fade into the chorus of all those you've ever cared about. And yet, when I read her on the page I'll know with certainty that brevity does not mitigate connection, that time does not prescribe importance.

The Indigo Girls concert is general admission, so we wake up early the next morning and camp out from ten in the morning in the freezing cold outside the Hofstra gym with a few other people from the Indigo Girls mailing list to get the front row. At first I think I'm doing this just to bond with everyone else while waiting, but when the show starts I know differently. I remember not just what it's like to see a show from the front row but what it's like to use my eyes again, to read people's faces not just

MAP   131

their words. I can learn so much just watching them. Amy's tight-muscled intensity during *Don't Give that Girl a Gun*. Emily's lit-up joy as the whole room sings *Galileo*. More than that. Watching Emily's face as Amy begins to play *Chickenman*, I can see a huge dynamic of their friendship, Emily recognizing the song as Amy's prayer, waiting with her whole being to feel Amy in that moment. I'm shaking and in tears. In Israel a few times I watched people connecting with God, and how that looked is how this feels.

Afterwards I know I have to try to thank them. The friend next to me is glowing. She's the one who knew what time to get to the gym and how we should dress so we wouldn't get frostbite waiting on line and where we could hear the soundcheck. I know she's planning to stay around. She says the three of us can crash with her again tonight and she can give us a ride to the train station in the morning. I look around for Tyler.

All around me people are yelling and reaching for guitar picks and copies of the setlist which are being tossed down at us by the road crew. I locate Tyler a few feet away but there are too many people. Heather sees me and smiles, and I gesture that I'll wait until the crowd thins. I'm just watching now, just so glad to be here. There's one setlist left. I see the guitar tech looking out at all the screamers, and the roadie with the setlist looks at the guitar tech who looks out directly at Tyler and points and says *her*. I look at Tyler's face, so appreciating, so understanding of the music and the joy, so deserving, and I'm amazed that the guitar tech could see it, too, but it feels right, and Tyler says *thank you* and the crowd starts to float away.

Tyler shows us the setlist, handwritten, abbreviations for some of the songs. She promises to make us all photocopies. She and Heather have to get back tonight, so we meet up with Tyler's friend who's driving them back and then part ways.

Waiting around all I can do is say the *Shehehiyanu,* the prayer for reaching this day, over and over. *Thank you God for me being alive.* Half a dozen fans are hanging around the gym, hoping the Indigo Girls will choose this door to get to their tour bus, hoping the security people are the nice kind. I'm a little further away, wandering around a stretch of empty parking lot, balancing on the curb, not wanting to disturb the moment with talk.

There was a question on the list last week, *what would you say if you met the Indigo Girls on an elevator?* An obsessed fan question, but also a question about fame and connection. My first response was that I would simply say *thank you,* but it didn't feel like enough, and then I remembered a line from an essay I'd written about Mary Chapin Carpenter a few years ago. *Sometimes a person touches your life from afar and it's enough just to be touched, but then there's this rare occasion when you need to reach out yourself. When she's shared so much of her life that the only way to say thank you is to introduce her to yours.* Back then it was just a question, *how? How would I convince her in the first thirty seconds that I'm worth knowing?* Today I'm pre-pared. On the trip up I made a little card for each of them, an invitation to visit the web site where I've begun to share my own art with the world, stories and essays and photographs.

I'm in my own zone, my music and my body rhythm. I hear voices as I balance along the curb, but I don't change my speed, don't look up until I reach the end and turn around. Fans have gathered in two clusters. I walk slowly towards one, enter. Amy's at my left elbow signing an autograph. She's tall. I wait, patiently, aware that I'm calm, aware that other fans are stum-bling breathless over their words, loan Amy a pen when hers runs out. I say my *thank you* hoping Amy can get the bigness of it from my voice and face, give her the card I made, and then move to the other cluster to wait for Emily.

Emily doesn't understand the card at first. It's small and she thinks I'm asking for an autograph, but I say *no, it's for you,* and she seems surprised but in a genuine grateful way. I say *thank you* and I can tell from her face that she knows I mean it, and I feel like in another plane of existence we might be friends.

When I get back to campus, Tyler asks *did you get me an autograph or anything?* She's so adorable asking the question that I don't know how to tell her I didn't even think of getting her one. It had seemed so odd to me that anyone had asked for an autograph—Amy and Emily had already given us so much. But Tyler looks so sincerely disappointed, even though she's trying to hide it, that I vow I'll make it up to her somehow.

I'm not sure how until a few weeks later, when we hear that the radio station Y100 is giving away free passes to an in-studio recording session. The Indigo Girls will play for about seventy people in a little room, and later the session will be broadcast on the radio. I have a good track record with winning things, and I decide that somehow Tyler is going to that show.

That night on the phone Tyler and I both listen to Y100 to find out the rules—be the fifth caller after such-and-such song—and then since we want to leave the phone lines free to call in, we continue listening while emailing back-and-forth. The station doesn't play the song, and doesn't play the song, and a couple of hours later the DJ repeats the rules and we realize that it's not happening tonight and that we both have class during the give-away time. But then the DJ says someone from the station will have a few passes to give away tomorrow between three-thirty and five at a place called Philly Rocks.

Tyler has class until five but mine ends earlier. I rush out of class at two forty-five and hop on the bus. I don't know exactly how to get to Philly Rocks. I know it's next to the UA Riverview theater, which isn't exactly bus accessible, so I get off the bus on the other side of the city as close as I can get to the Delaware River, but I'm confused. I ask questions, ask more questions, keep checking my watch. Time is running out. I reach the river and don't know whether to go left or right or what to do after that, so I go into this little Irish store and the woman behind the counter tells me how to get there, draws me a whole map. I say *thank you thank you, you are helping to hopefully make someone very happy,* and decide I'll go back later and buy something if I do get the passes, and then I follow the directions, running, through traffic on broken sidewalk next to a highway, *no wonder you can't take public transportation here,* and I get to Philly Rocks at three-thirty on the dot expecting a mob and no one else is there.

I ask the first person I see, who directs me to someone else, who directs me to someone else, and I wait around while he finishes talking and then introduce myself, talking fast fast because I'm still out of breath from running. *I'm-Audrey-and-I-have-this-friend-Tyler-and-she's-just-the-greatest-best-person-and-if-you-do-this-you-could-make-her-so-happy-and-if-anyone-should-be-there-it's-Tyler-and-I-don't-usually-ask-for-things-I-wouldn't-do-it-for-me-it's-for-sister-love-and-I'm-graduating-if-not-now-when* and so on and so forth *and-so-you-would-be-doing-the-greatest-mitzvah-that's-Hebrew-for-good-deed-if-you-could-just-give-me-two-passes-to-the-Indigo-Girls-recording-session-next-week,* and he grins and says, *you want Indigo Girls passes? Sure. Enjoy!* And I say *thank you* as big as I can and my face breaks into a huge smile, and I say I'm going to write a book about all this someday, and

MAP   135

I'll put him in, and then I sit down and order some nachos and something to drink and find a quarter and ask the waitress where the pay phone is.

And then I call Tyler and say to her in a really really calm nonchalant voice, *whatever plans you have for April fifteenth, you'll have to change them, because we're going to the Y100 Indigo Girls recording session.* And hearing the excitement in Tyler's voice is more of a reward than passes to a recording session could ever be.

Just Between Us

April is about hanging out on College Green, coming out of indoor hibernation and seeing everyone else at Penn who's been hibernating all winter. Today I spend a lazy afternoon lying out there on the grass with my new crush, Hope, other friends coming and going. The sun is shining and the lawn is covered with people. My freshman roommate stops to say hello on her way to class. The cute boy I met at the lesbigay association meeting I attended last week with Tyler passes by and waves. Dormmates play frisbee across the way. I see writer friends from my first Penn fiction workshop, people I know from Hillel and from AJ's a cappella group, my editor from the yearbook, an acquaintance I haven't seen since studying in Israel last year. I see a lot of exposed skin, bare feet and sandals, shorts and short sleeves and tank tops. It's spring again.

I watch Hope as she talks to these two guys, responds to their flirtations. She reminds me of Sasha a little—her whole personality is cute, in that confident flirty artsy crunchy way that seems to be equally attractive to both men and women. Although she likes both, too, she's not out, so I don't join the guys in flirting with her, even though I want to. When they aren't looking, Hope gives me a wink. I think about something Matthew said, how eighty percent of communication is non-verbal. I decide

MAP   137

not to ever email Hope. I know I'm braver over email, and I want whatever happens or doesn't to take place in person. I had a platonic date with her last Sunday, a meal at a nice restaurant and the kind of long conversation that feels like a date, a good date—attraction and flirtation—but no kissing and I'm not sure if Hope would call it a date but it was *something*. It's too close to graduation to really pursue something with her, but it's fun to feel this way again.

Nice article, Matthew says, stopping by with a newspaper containing my *Relativity* article under his arm. *I like the pseudonym.* After weighing my dad's counsel, I had ultimately chosen to publish the article in the *Daily Pennsylvanian*'s annual gay supplement using the pseudonym *Henry Beatitudes,* which is an anagram of my name.

That was you? Hope asks. *Rock on.*

Matthew people-watches with us for a while. *He's family,* Matthew says, pointing out a guy in a cluster of frat guys. He uses the term *family* to mean *not heterosexual.*

What's his name? I ask.

Matthew shrugs, pointing out another couple of people. *She's a dyke,* he says. *And he's definitely gay.*

The guy is our campus homosexual poster boy, but I've never seen the woman before. *How do you know?* I ask.

If you're not sure, Matthew says, *watch their eyes, who they're looking at, particularly when they think no one's watching.*

But I look at everyone, I say.

Matthew just laughs.

In the evening Whitney from Seattle calls me up. *How are you?* she asks.

Great, I say, truly meaning it.

I guess I shouldn't tell you then, she says. From her voice I know it's about Catrina and another woman.

Don't, I say.

You'll feel better knowing, Whitney says, but I'm not convinced. *She fell in love,* that's what I expect to hear. I can picture Catrina with someone really cute, someone I would want, and I'd rather not know. Whitney's already said too much. It would be easier if I didn't know anyone who knew Catrina, if I could just imagine this part and leave it be.

We play the should-she-tell-me game for a while. It's a catch-22. If she doesn't, I'll keep agonizing. Finally I let Whitney tell me. *You know Penny?* she says.

Yeah. Penny is another person from the Indigo Girls mailing list, someone Catrina thought was hot and had had a crush on. She's older, thirty-four or something. I once saw her picture on someone's web page and didn't get why Catrina was attracted to her.

Well, she and Catrina were all over each other at the Indigo Girls show. I mean all over.

At least it's someone I've heard about. It's not like she found a new unknown perfect soulmate. I guess I feel relief, but then that goes away and I don't know how I feel, numb and bad, complex bad, not simple bad but twisted. Distant.

I don't want to be angry, I say.

Anger's a good thing, Whitney says. *I'm surprised it's taken you this long to feel it. She's a jerk. You deserve better.*

I borrow a guitar from someone down the hall I don't know, an electric guitar. I've never played electric. Now I just sit on his couch and try to get it all out without breaking the guitar. Talk a little. Somehow talking helps, telling someone who doesn't

MAP   139

know, where I can just say my ex is seeing someone else. No long story about email or woman or anything, just *my ex who left me in order to be alone found someone new.*

I can't play this guitar forever. I swear I'm going to get my own again soon, a five dollar variety that I can play in the rain, smash to bits if I need to. Instead I go back to my room. I blast the most angry bitter music I can find in my entire CD collection, and then go for a bike ride. Pedal fast. I can't take the distance, I can't take the distance. Why did Catrina take the coward's way out, break up with me over email, not even have the decency to use the phone? Just cut me off. She never paid me back for the Dar Williams tickets either. They were on my credit card and she used them, took some friend, and never paid me back.

What if I had insisted on going to see Catrina in February, rather than gamble on some distant friendship possibility, some feeble hope? I feel so alone right now, so much more alone than I did before I had a taste of what *not alone* meant, more alone than when Catrina first broke my heart. How could she abandon me so completely like this? How could she say all those things about needing to be alone with her self-absorption and then turn around so soon to be with someone else?

I kick at the pedals, grip the handlebars, feel the whole bike swerve. Did she—when did it *start?* No. Don't think about that. Don't go there. There's no way to really know the truth.

Look forward. Keep the bike moving steady. Keep your skin off the asphalt.

Already in my mind I can't see Catrina alone anymore. I see her now with this other woman, I see her joking and making fun of me and she will have forgotten, the emails might have been deleted, might still be at her fingertips, does her promise still mean anything? *That is just between us,* she promised me about those emails, *and it will be something we will always have, and share.* I want to break the promise, show the world, betray her so she can't betray me.

I'm mad, thinking to myself *what good does anger do?* and still feeling it, anger and loneliness, and I try to hold onto it because I know if I don't, if I let go, this whole thing will continue fading. What happened to the woman I fell in love with? To the woman who said *until we meet, and know for sure, you have my heart?* I remember what Whitney said in Seattle about meeting Catrina, and I wonder, what if the Catrina I knew only existed with me, only existed during that short time we were both in love with each other?

I keep pedaling, block after block, and the anger goes away. It will come back, as will the disappointment, as will the loss. This bike ride will not resolve for good the tangled web of feelings and uneven growth and new confidence and insecurities brought about by my relationship with Catrina. But for the moment, as I bike past Thirtieth Street, the anger is gone. And as I cross the bridge over the Schuylkill River, coasting towards downtown, I find myself sincerely, surprisingly, unselfishly, happy for Catrina.

I pedal on past Rittenhouse Square, lighter, and into another feeling, a desire for something physical, sexual. Something physical from someone else so that Catrina won't be getting ahead of me. I imagine running into Catrina in Seattle, bumping into her and Penny when I'm least prepared. I imagine a summer spent trying to avoid interaction. I don't want to be around Catrina next summer feeling so vulnerable, knowing that she's way past me and the balance is gone and there's nowhere for us to connect. I still want to go to Seattle but not like that. Not this soon. I don't want to be so far from home, so far from a hug, and be hurting.

MAP   141

I'm really feeling the limitations of email, of its lack of touch. During the breakup aftermath I didn't touch anyone until Professor Snow hugged me, afraid I guess of losing control. Of letting a moment of weakness propel me into another yucky situation like the tutor or a rebound where I became the one inflicting hurt. As much as I've cried about Catrina, I've only let myself when I'm alone, and I feel like there's something in me still waiting for a safe place to be small.

That weekend I'll hear from mutual friend Heidi, *Catrina swears that nothing physical happened between her and Penny while you two were emailing.* I'll choose to believe this. I'll try not to think about the realm of possibilities behind *nothing physical,* and for the most part, I'll succeed, at least until much later in life when I receive an education in the wide murky spectrum of infidelity.

All evening I think about everything that's not email. I think about Amy and Emily on stage, about Tyler's voice when I got the Y100 passes, about AJ giving me a makeover, about Hope. I open the window and listen to the sounds of sirens, planes, people. I feel the breeze. I smell meat cooking down the hall and incense wafting through the heating vent.

I think about people saying *I thought I was in love but I was wrong.* What if Catrina says it? What if Catrina says it, she's with Penny or someone else and she says, *oh that with Audrey, that was nothing.*

That's the part I hate most, right there. Everyone else can say it doesn't count—I can take that. They don't know. But what if Catrina does? What if I write about us and Catrina reads it and laughs it off, she reads it aloud to Penny making jokes to distance herself, to deny that it mattered? Can that negate what happened?

Jay was my boyfriend the summer after fourth grade. We dared each other to kiss on the lips over and over that summer on my front porch swing, made lemonade ice cubes together and wrote each other letters we hid in the secret hiding place underneath the porch steps. Then I went to sleepaway camp after sixth grade and Paul asked me out. Paul and I never kissed but we skipped stones by the camp lake and I told my parents that I had a boyfriend, and he became my first boyfriend—Jay just got erased because I wanted Paul to be my first boyfriend. The next summer I thought Paul was an immature jerk and broke up with him.

I think about Jake again. I envision a photograph, *Everyman and Everywoman*. Growing old together, sorting bills, making love with tender familiar imperfections. Could that be me? Is Jake the one that got away?

Now when I look back Paul wasn't such a jerk, just a picked-on kid who acted too much like a flaming queen, and Jay was my first boyfriend again. Jay had two other girlfriends at the same time, but I was the only one who would kiss him on the lips. And I remember when I was ten on Jay's birthday I found out you could have sex without babies, if you weren't getting your period yet, and I wanted to go over to Jay's and ask *let's try it*. And I did go over, but his brothers were there so I was too scared to ask, and now I wonder, *what if I had, what if it had happened?* If I'd been able to know all these years, *I had sex*, been able to pull that out like a hidden ace instead of having the insecurity of *everyone's farther along?* Could it have erased the tutor somehow? Made things less scary with Jake? Helped me come out to myself sooner than I did? How would it have changed the rest?

MAP   143

The next time I hear from Catrina, it will be a stiffly-worded email asking me to delete her name from where it appears on my website. She'll send a similar request to Tyler, then shut down her email account and disappear from the internet entirely, and after that I won't hear from her for nearly a decade, when I seek her out—a challenge in itself—and via email I offer to show her the memoir I've written. *Please change my name,* she'll request. *A lot of people in my life don't know about....* And I will finally wonder in earnest, what drew *her* to the email world? What was she trying to hide or to find?

But her story, I will realize, is not mine to tell, nor mine to know. I will feel grateful for whatever it is that has given me words for my own experiences and that provides me with the strength to share them. I will hope she has found peace in her silence.

I Kissed a Girl

I meet Jenn and her girlfriend in the parking lot after an Indigo Girls show. They're leaning together against a beaten-up, bumper-stickered hatchback. Jenn is wearing a baseball cap over her nearly-shaved head, her girlfriend Ann-Marie has not-so-short-but-still-short hair and a choker-style hemp necklace, they look like a couple, they look like they've never seen the closet, they look like what I expected Tyler and Heather to look like that first time. Dykes.

We're waiting for the sea of cars to clear out before leaving. Jenn pulls out her guitar and I try to play it and then she plays for a while. She's better than me, which isn't hard. Two weeks ago I graduated, and three days ago I moved to Boston, and now I'm surrounded by Jenn and Ann-Marie and my new roommate and a bunch of other people from the Indigo Girls list, all these dykes, and tomorrow we're all going to Boston Pride. *Tomorrow's my first Gay Pride,* I say, and Jenn says *mine too* and I ask *when did you come out?* and she says *October* and we high-five. I look around and it feels like I've really *arrived* somewhere, like these

MAP   145

are the people I envied last summer when I saw the Indigo Girls at the Newport Folk Festival and now I'm part of it.

My new roommate invited Jenn and her girlfriend to crash at our place for the weekend, since they're here from Maine, so I drive back with them to show the way and my roommate goes in the other car. Ann-Marie drives and Jenn and I try to include her in the conversation, but mostly she just listens.

Jenn tells me about getting her head shaved, and how it's all scratchy and she wishes it would grow back in already. I tell Jenn about the show at Hofstra. We talk about how it's really possible to get to know someone through lyrics and music and watching her face onstage, not completely of course but the really deep important parts. We talk about writing because Jenn does it too, and about what it would be like to go to Atlanta where the Indigo Girls started. I find out that Jenn is four years younger than I am, so it's eerie the way we're clicking, the way her mind works. It's like talking to myself at a younger age.

When we get back, I pull out the red three-ring binder where I keep my stories. While Jenn and Ann-Marie are reading my new stuff, I turn to the front of the binder and occupy myself by rereading a short story I wrote in high school. It's about two male best friends in boarding school during the seventies, and in the pivotal scene, after an awkward wrestling match in the locker room that leaves them both aroused, Neil comes out to Brian. I reach the line *Doubts over whether he was straight or not still existed in Brian's head, but he knew that he was definitely turned on by women.* I reread it aloud.

I completely forgot I wrote that, I say. *Brian is the name I would have had if I was a boy.*

Jenn is wowed by the first story I give her, and then she

asks to read the high school story and she's impressed by that too, and it feels good to have new friends reading my stuff. My roommate and I set up blankets on the floor for the two of them and say good night. I go in my room and close my door and wonder what Jenn and Ann-Marie are doing, would they have sex in someone else's living room, and in the morning we wake up and go to Boston Pride.

A couple of days later Jenn emails me, *Ann-Marie and I are over with, we'd broken up once before but had the tickets already and there's just something about being with someone on Pride day.* We email once or twice and then Wednesday on the phone she says she's bored and I say *come to Boston* so the next morning she does.

We buy tickets in Harvard Square to see *Chasing Amy* but there are a couple of hours until the show, so we stop by Tower Records. The latest edition of the free *Pulse* magazine has Amy and Emily on the cover. We take a couple and joke about taking them all, and then sit on the ledge outside by the travel agency with the *Please Go Away* sign and read the article. This girl comes out of Tower with a bag, and from the shape of it I say *it's gotta be Pulse magazines, and why else would she have that many if she's not an obsessed Indigo Girls fan?* She sits down on the grass across the street for a while to look and when she gets back up Jenn calls to her, *do you like the Indigo Girls?* She comes over and says *yes,* and we talk and she's all impressed because we have bootlegs of a few of the early shows. Later we pass by Tower Records again. I tell Jenn, *wait a sec,* and I run in and grab a whole pack. The magazines are bundled in plastic, so the pack is easy to carry, and we run and we count them in Herrell's Ice Cream and there are twenty-five copies. We'll send them to all

MAP   147

the people on the list who live in Hicksville, USA, but until then we don't want to carry them around, so we find a back alley driveway to store them until after the movie.

In the movie Jenn is cold, so I put my arm around her, and she reaches her left hand up and takes mine, and it's nice. Walking back, I carry the *Pulses* in one hand and hold her hand with the other and I think how cool it is that it's safe to do this in Cambridge, Massachusetts, and it feels like we've really become good friends in less than a week. Back home I shower and then she does while I set up the blankets in the living room again. My roommate's sleeping or I think she is, but she left the radio playing blues and her door is open so we try to be quiet. When Jenn gets out of the shower I go to give her a good night hug but it doesn't end.

We're dancing in the living room real slow, and then we go to switch positions so my chin would be on her left shoulder instead of her right, and her eyes are closed and our lips brush. I know then it's gonna happen. We keep dancing for a while no rush then slowly back to the middle and we're kissing and I open my eyes and look at her. This feels familiar, like I've done it with a woman before and just forgot, and I wonder if I have, maybe with Sasha as kids or something, but it's just that kissing is kissing.

Her tongue is shorter than I thought and kind of triangular as it reaches. She laughs a little and says she was thinking about what she'll tell her best friend, when he asks why she broke up with Ann-Marie. *What?* I ask, and she says, *this chick's writing.* She kisses me and I don't say anything and I kiss her back and play with her hair which is just starting to grow back, it's fuzzy and feels neat between my fingers. After a while she says *it's getting late* and then I take her hands and gesture towards my room. *I don't want to go too far,* she says, *I've regretted things before,* and I promise that we won't, thinking to myself *I don't want it to go too far any more than she does,* but I don't want to say that, I don't want her to know she's the first girl I've kissed. So I just squeeze her hands, and I guess my promise is good, because she follows me in.

Epilogue

I remember a Shabbat afternoon at camp, the summer I was sixteen. Knocking on the door of bunk 58, the bunk of Noah Edelman, my Tom Cruise look-alike counselor. My friend Jon answered, got Noah for me. Noah and I talked on the bench outside his bunk. I forget what about. God maybe. Some religion question I might or might not have concocted to get his attention. I didn't really have a crush or whatever it was on Noah anymore, not like I had for the previous two summers, but he was still part of my confused adolescent dynamic of being at camp. Which is to say, I still wanted him to want me—to want my mind and want my body too, to desire me, to fall for me, to lead the rest of the hot guys at camp into wanting me that way. I still sent him Shabbat-o-grams sometimes and still debated whether to sign them *love*.

You know Jon? Noah asked as he stood on the steps of his cabin, hand on the doorhandle, about to head in even though I wanted to talk to him longer. *Would you go out with him?*

He's not my type, I said.

Maybe Noah asked what my type was, or maybe he just asked the question I distinctly remember. *Am I your type, Audge?*

Another camper was approaching the bunk, almost within earshot, and someone else was calling Noah's name from inside.

Kind of, I said, adding quickly as he turned to go in, *but you're a counselor so I'm trying to forget it.*

I didn't hear what he responded, if he responded.

What if I was bolder back then? *Yes, you're my type. Am I yours?* Cornered him later if I had to, demanded an answer.

Does it matter? Would it have made a difference, having that answer? Would the answer itself have mattered?

It does go back to age ten with Jay, but not the way I used to believe. I mean, even if I'd asked Jay, *let's try it,* what are the chances we would have actually had sex? More likely, he would have said no—scared of his brothers, afraid of getting caught, preferring to ride bikes, whatever. I've shaped that scene in my memory like having an early sexual experience with a childhood friend would have been the magic answer, but the truth is that this is the earliest memory I have of fear getting the best of me. It's not about sex. It's about losing and gaining the confidence to ask for what I want, to name my desires and my limits, to hold my ground. It's about learning to communicate.

* * *

In the months after coming out to my parents and moving to Boston, I become frustrated by my father's silences whenever Mom and I are talking about gaydar or my volunteer work on the Bisexual Resource Guide or her donations to P-FLAG and the Lambda legal fund for gay rights. I make an effort to respect my father's comfort level, but I hate having to watch every single thing I say at family gatherings, for fear that I will out myself to some cousin by accident, and word will get back to my grandparents who will be upset about hearing it third-hand.

MAP   151

In November, I announce to my parents that I am tired of not being *out* to my extended family, and I insist that my father tell my grandparents for me.

My father is adamantly opposed to the idea, insisting that Grandma and Grandpa don't need to know, and that if it is that important to me, then I should tell them myself, but my mom takes my side.

I tell my father that he can figure out when and how to do it in a way that feels comfortable to him, but that I am not going to another family gathering where I have to shut up and feel uncomfortable, and if that meant missing tomorrow's post-Thanksgiving family festivities, so be it, and if that means missing Passover as well, so be it, although I really hope that won't happen. He insists I go. I refuse to back down. *Fine, Mommy and I will go,* he says.

If Audrey is staying home, I am staying home, my mother says.

Then I won't go either, my father says, well into stubborn mode by then. I tell him that if he isn't going, he should plan to go somewhere else tomorrow, because I don't want to see him. *Whose house is this?* my father demands.

My mom thinks I have gone too far, that I can't kick my father out of his own house. In my frustration I don't think it is such an unreasonable demand. But the next morning Dad heads to the post-Thanksgiving family festivities and Mom and I stay home, and when Dad comes back from New York, he surprises us both by saying, *I told them.*

As long as she's happy, my grandpa told him, *that's what we care about,* and my grandma said, *I guess that's the style these days,* which is what she said to me when I wore pants to synagogue on Rosh Hashanah. Later, my grandma will corner me in her tiny kitchen and ask, *so tell me, are you still bi-seks-ual?* and

I will tell her about Catrina and how she broke my heart and Grandma will hug me tight.

It's a good thing both my parents died before you came out, my mom tells me. *We probably wouldn't be speaking to them anymore. I'm sure they're rolling over in their graves.*

Later, much much later, I will share this manuscript with my parents. My mom will cry every time she reads the chapter called *What It Is to Lose a Zoe.*

I guess there isn't anyone else who will see that chapter exactly the way I see it, she'll tell me. *It makes me cry because the person I love most in the world was hurting, and it makes me cry because I wasn't there to hug you and you didn't even tell me about it until it was in the past. I am glad that Professor Snow was there for you. She is a special lady.*

* * *

I'm settled in Boston, single and *on the make,* as my friend Deb calls it. She directs me through the PlanetOut.com personals like she's my Driver's Ed teacher, pointing, *go here, click there, not that one, click on her, yes. Email her. Right now.*

No, I say, pausing the game. *You have your own relationship. Stop trying to live vicariously through me.* But the woman in the photo is cute and her ad intrigues me, so I bookmark the page.

Later that week, I feel a window of courage. I email PlanetOut Girl quickly before I get too nervous or longwinded. *Saw your ad, like your writing style and your humor, I'm a twenty-something writer* blah blah blah *email me back and I'll say more and maybe eventually we can go on a date.*

She responds. I respond. A couple more rounds back and forth. PlanetOut Girl's email persona is reminding me of Catrina

MAP   153

magnified. The exclamation points and *tee hee*'s are a little much and I'm not quite feeling a click, but there's an adrenaline rush with each email and her picture is cute and she's funny and all her vital stats are decent—she's studying to be a teacher, writing a screen play, so on and so forth, we'll have stuff to talk about. She's probably going to move somewhere else when she gets out of grad school but I'm not thinking this is the love of my life anyway. I'm only using the internet as a more comfortable alternative to *come here often?*

I want to be damn sure of a meeting this time.

PlanetOut Girl's favorite food is *ICE CREAM, BABY!!!!!* so I suggest an ice cream date.

We meet for ice cream. She looks different from her picture, a little older, still cute but the disconnect is enough to throw me off. Conversation's a little awkward, not horrible, not particularly interesting. Half an hour into the date I need to pee and I excuse myself to go to the bathroom. When I get back, Planet Out Girl is standing up, offering someone else our table. I ask if she wants to wander around for a while, but it's clear the date is over and the fifteen minutes we spend in a nearby bookstore don't change that fact. The date clocks in at roughly forty-nine minutes, my shortest ever.

As I drive back home, it occurs to me that if Catrina and I had met up like this, maybe it would have come to naught. If she'd lived on campus like Tyler and joined us to watch Indigo Girls videos, we might not even have experienced an initial click. Even if we'd fallen in love on email first and then flown to meet each other the next day, it could have fizzled instantaneously in a flash of *not what I expected*. An in-person flash of *not what I expected* followed by forty-nine minutes of conversation with no click, and we might have given up.

Bless the internet, then. Bless the internet and the phone for bringing us so close. For giving us a chance.

Although I didn't see it at the time, and I'm still not quite sure, I think our relationship changed when I bought the plane ticket, and I guess Catrina wasn't ready for what that ticket meant. I do have some faith that if she hadn't freaked out, an in-person relationship could have worked out for a little while, that we would have gotten through the awkward disconnect, reassuring ourselves, *maybe she looks different but this is the woman I'm in love with, give it time, we just need to get to know each other in this new way.* But eventually it would have come to an end, if for no other reason than that what I'm looking for now in a partner doesn't match up with the person she was or the person she was trying to become.

There are words I'd almost forgotten that I wrote, *you know you're in love when you're willing to have a kid and a dog and move to Washington for her.* In a way, it doesn't matter if it happens or not, if you realize it too late, if she feels the same way. The lovestory's not in the beginning of the attraction, and it's not in the ending of the relationship, it's in that one moment when what's most important shifts.

A part of me still loves Catrina, and always will, but her as she was, with me as I was. When the mere sound of her voice would make me wish I could start walking with the phone as we talked, meet her halfway in the middle of the continent. Time passes and she fades, and I wonder how much was just circumstance, us being young and new to a world and never in love before. How much was just about sharing these new emotions together. How much was just us hoping it would work.

We had wedding outfits picked out, me in ripped jeans, her in overalls, and a flower girl in combat boots with lace. I thought

MAP   155

about dancing at our wedding. It was the first time I ever thought about dancing with a woman, and for years, every time I thought of dancing, I was left reaching for her. The feeling of loss was a feeling of all that should have happened first with her and won't, and yet when it starts to happen, it feels like it already has.

Her legacy is this sense of imbalance, this sense that when love happens across three thousand miles, it leaves something aching in its wake. We learned together that being intimate isn't about being physical, it's about erasing the distance between people. I carry that lesson with me, yet I still wish Catrina and I had been able to look into each other's eyes, taste each other's skin.

I was left trying to explain this, explain us, explain her. I was left defensive, *this relationship counts,* doubting myself, seeking validation, secretly wondering what it was that so many people seemed to think I missed. I began writing, my early drafts filled with the omission and half-truths of someone trying to prove something she couldn't quite trust. Over time, the writing process itself guided me through. I learned to make peace with uncertainty. I noticed that even those people who seemed to think that this relationship didn't quite count still responded to individual passages of manuscript, *yes, I remember that feeling, I've been there.* I moved on into and out of other loves, each one adding layers of topography to the map you now hold in your hands. Over time, the map will continue changing.

THANK YOU

To the pseudonymous Catrina

To Amy and Emily, for the music

To Lorene and Karen, for teaching and caring

To Laurette, for the gift of my first coming out

To Preston, for the Indigo Girls passes

To my many readers of Map-in-progress, for feedback and encouragement, and to everyone who's believed in me along the way, with extra-special thanks to Drew, Janice, Deb, Susan, Holly, Dan, Patricia, Nate, Linda, Nicole, Julie, Nathan, Dorie, Book Group, Erin, Kate, Matthew, Amber, Althea, T. Lee, Jacob, Mara, Jason, Joan, Deb, Sherry, Debbie, Grace, Doug, Jessica, Robyn, Sheeri, Sara, Sara, Cristie, Solma, Nicole, Pete, Karen, Dave, Raphael, Andi, Alex, Andy, Jen, Brenda, Brams, Karen, and my family

To all the writers and musicians who have inspired me
and given me something to strive for

For the second edition

THANK YOU to the many friends and family who have helped me grow from 2009 to now and who have brought me safely through two years of pandemic. To Art Night and Quite Write, for holding the creative space. And to Laurette, Kate, and Sam, whose conversations and witness helped me articulate anew and become ready to release a more comfortably-boundaried version of this story to the world.

A NOTE ABOUT THE SECOND EDITION

This edition began with a thought that kept reappearing. A question, really. What it might be like to revisit *Map*.

I wondered whether there was a way to offer my now-self to my then-self, not as author but as editor and sage and protector. To publish the book I wish I'd have had the wisdom and the self-care to publish in 2009, rather than the one that actually existed.

There was only one way to find out, and it led me here.

I cut out things that I'd put into early drafts of *Map* thinking I had to, and hadn't learned until after I published that it was okay to keep private. I also rewrote sentences and paragraphs to more accurately portray power dynamics and culpability while not retraumatizing myself or readers. I changed, added, or deleted just over a thousand words in total, yet these choices were as significant as every word that is included in *Map*.

The first edition accurately captured some dynamics that I couldn't actually see until well after it was published. Most notably in the chapters where I come out to my parents. That's a story for another time and place, and I kept those sections of the book as-is, but it feels important to acknowledge. When I read those chapters now, I want to shower then-Audrey with unconditional love. I want to tell her that she has a right to privacy, boundaries, respect, and her own timeline—no matter what.

I also want to acknowledge these lines in the chapter called If I'm Falling Down, "A relationship not working out is something I can grasp. Feelings changing is something I can't." *Feelings changing is something I can't.* Hard to fathom now. My margin note to my then-self is this: "Oh dear one. I just want to squeeze you safe and tight."